# MASTERING YOUR MENTAL GAME

# MASTERING YOUR MENTAL GAME

### A Practical Guide to Improving Your
### Performance in Sports, Work and Life

## JULIE ELION

**SIMON &
SCHUSTER**

London · New York · Amsterdam/Antwerp · Sydney/Melbourne · Toronto · New Delhi

First published in the United States by Avid Reader Press,
an imprint of Simon & Schuster, LLC, 2026

First published in Great Britain by Simon & Schuster UK Ltd, 2026

1 3 5 7 9 10 8 6 4 2

Simon & Schuster UK Ltd
1st Floor
222 Gray's Inn Road
London WC1X 8HB

www.simonandschuster.co.uk
www.simonandschuster.com.au
www.simonandschuster.co.in

Simon & Schuster Australia, Sydney
Simon & Schuster India, New Delhi

The authorised representative in the EEA is Simon & Schuster Netherlands BV,
Herculesplein 96, 3584 AA Utrecht, Netherlands. info@simonandschuster.nl

A CIP catalogue record for this book is available from the British Library

Hardback ISBN: 978-1-3985-5250-0
Trade Paperback ISBN: 978-1-3985-5251-7
eBook ISBN: 978-1-3985-5252-4

Book text design by Paul Dippolito

Printed and Bound in the UK using 100% Renewable Electricity at CPI Group (UK) Ltd

*This book is dedicated to Tim Rosaforte.*

# Contents

# MASTERING YOUR MENTAL GAME

# Chapter 1

# Digging Deep

*"Be not afraid of growing slowly, be afraid of standing still."*
—Ancient Chinese proverb

By the time Wyndham Clark stood in the 18th fairway at Los Angeles Country Club, the light over the city of angels was low, and I had worked my way around to the green to try to best get a glimpse of my client trying to close out the 2023 U.S. Open. It was a Sunday evening, the final round. The galleries were huge and boisterous. Rory McIlroy had just gotten to the clubhouse at 9 under par. Wyndham stood at 10 under, a par from his first major championship.

Our path to this point was both methodical and remarkably fast. Wyndham and I first met only six months earlier, in December 2022. By that time, I had spent more than a quarter century working on the PGA Tour and with golfers from around the world on their mental approach. Wyndham was initially skeptical that working with a coach to help him control his thoughts would help him actually win tournaments. "You guys all say the same things," he told me when we first met. "Nothing works." He was saying the same things to his team—his caddie, his agent—even though those closest to him believed what I had to offer could help him unlock his potential, which was enormous.

That's not an atypical reaction, and it could be the same for people picking up this book: How could talking with someone—or reading about how to control our thoughts and emotions—produce better golf shots, lower scores, and better results? Is it psychobabble? Even with all my experience on tour—and all the success my clients have had, more than 25 majors and 120 PGA Tour victories—I run into those doubts all the time.

Wyndham's reluctance eventually waned. In February 2023, we met at a Starbucks near his home in Scottsdale, Arizona. Shortly thereafter, we started meeting by Zoom every week. We put in place some of the tools I'll outline in this book, tools that can help a struggling golfer on the PGA Tour but could also help anyone on any course in any circumstance—playing for a club championship or a weekly Nassau with buddies.

Over the ensuing weeks, Wyndham started to feel better about himself, and his golf improved. This wasn't a straight line, and you'll discover in the coming pages that the journey to better golf—just like the road to a better life—is almost never linear. In March, he was within a shot of the lead entering the final round of a tournament in the Dominican Republic, but he played the back nine of the final round 1 over par to fall into a tie for sixth. That kind of slip used to eat him up. We needed to figure out how to push him forward, and to help him believe good things were going to happen in his future.

"If we had a crystal ball in our lives—which we don't—you'd know why this loss is important," I told him. "We've got to use this setback as a positive, because you don't know what's going to happen the next day. What we do know: You're better than this and will win soon."

Just more than a month later, he beat a terrific field to win the Wells Fargo Championship, his first PGA Tour win! My reaction that day (and his): This stuff works.

Now, it's important to note very early in this long discussion: Self-improvement—be it in golf or in life—isn't always going to be on a smooth, upward trajectory. In fact, it's most often not. Our highest highs can be followed by some pretty low lows. Wyndham Clark took a long time to begin examining his life, and my belief is he was rewarded for doing so. But for any of us, this is a process.

Golfers don't reach the top and then stay there forever. Our own golf games can go through extraordinary ups and downs. Any golf fan knows that Wyndham's 2025 season was rocky, marred by inconsistent play on the course and some unflattering incidents off it. At the PGA Championship, he hurled his driver in anger following an errant tee shot, snapping off the head and nearly hitting a volunteer. At the U.S. Open, he took his frustrations out on a locker in the Oakmont Country Club clubhouse. Mastering our mental game in golf or reaching a state of growth and self-improvement in life isn't always a permanent condition. It takes more work over more years, and there are frequently hills and valleys.

But back in 2023, with the U.S. Open just more than a month away, Wyndham and I began talking more profoundly and thoroughly about everything that makes him who he is. We began digging deep.

•   •   •

One of my favorite quotes—a quote that gets to the heart of my work—is from Socrates: "The unexamined life is not worth living."

There are plenty of great athletes and successful executives who go about their professional and personal lives without the kind of introspection Socrates refers to. For the most part, the people who avoid introspection aren't going to stick with me once we start our work—or come to me at all in the first place—because they come to understand, quite quickly, that our journey involves self-examination. Very deep self-examination.

That doesn't start with, "Well, on the first hole I drove it in the left rough and made bogey, and on the third I nailed my tee shot to the center of the green but three-putted." We all have conversations like this, where they describe their shots as if I were their caddie. Sometimes it's after a round. Sometimes it's at a party. I can feel my eyelids getting heavy. Can't you?

Rather, the people who come to me—whether they're golfers, businesspeople, or athletes from any sport—arrive first with a curiosity about themselves and what might help make them better performers. Second, they come with a commitment to grow.

Combine that curiosity with commitment, and what they're showing is a willingness to dig deep. My nickname on the PGA Tour used to be "Stealth," because I worked quietly around the edges of tournaments with a wide array of clients, some of whom were comfortable being associated with me in public, many of whom preferred our relationship to be private. Either is fine. Discretion—particularly twenty-five years ago, when fewer people publicly addressed their mental health—is part of the job.

A newer nickname, though, cuts closer to what I do. In recent years, one of the physical therapists who works with players and is part of the tour's traveling circus began referring to me as "Backhoe." The reason: I dig deep. Every one of us has a past that's worth mining. When I begin talking with a client, we work to excavate all the material that's under the surface, history that can prevent anyone from becoming their best as a golfer or being their best selves. We might not know what we'll find. It might not be pretty. It could be scary. But people don't come to me or stay with me unless they know—consciously or not—they want to dig deep.

There's a quote from Brian D. Mahan, an expert in releasing stress and trauma from the body, that appeals to me and relates to what I do: "You can go to the gym, drink your water and take your vitamins, but if you don't deal with the crap going on in your own heart and head, you're still going to be unhealthy."

It's so true, and it touches not just on golf, but on any pursuit at work or at home. So many athletes and businesspeople think, "If I go, 'Check, check, check, check,' and cross off a bunch of small items, I'm accomplishing what I need to, and I'll be fine." But if they don't look at how their father criticized their results if they made a bogey, or made them wash the kitchen floor if they played a lousy round—true stories I know from the tour—then what's the point? Where are we going? What are we getting out of it?

Here's something I encounter all the time—not on the PGA Tour, but among regular folks I know. So many people play golf—even somewhat regularly, like maybe a few times a week—but don't put in time to practice and work on their games. And then so many of those same people get angry when they don't improve. They're frustrated. They're slamming clubs. They're storming from the 18th green to the parking lot because their 85 from last Saturday didn't magically turn into a 78 a week later.

Isn't that wild? Complain, complain, complain, but don't work on improving? If you have a vegetable garden because you like being in the soil, but you don't know anything about what you're doing, should you complain and get frustrated when your tomatoes die or your lettuce doesn't grow? No. You read about how to best tend to them, work at putting best practices in place, water and fertilize them properly. It takes effort.

So does golf. I always say to these people, "If you don't want to get better at this game, but you still want to play, that's great. Go have fun. Go hit it around and do your thing. Be unconscious or conscious about it. That's your choice."

But if you really want to improve, it takes work. It takes curiosity. It takes a commitment to getting better not only at the mechanics of the swing. It takes knowing yourself. It takes digging deep.

I've worked with players who have both lived as well as played their sport. I've worked with players who took their talent for granted until they ran into an injury, then discovered what hard work was really like. The commitment to getting better, though, can apply to almost anything. What are you curious about yourself—on or off the course? Maybe you want to be a better communicator. Maybe you want to do a better job separating your professional life from your personal life. Maybe you want to be able to appreciate experiences more acutely without allowing stress and troubles to get in the way. There's almost no limit to what we can explore. Wyndham has continued to learn how to balance and focus his emotions. Seeking higher degrees of mental health and resilience is a lifelong journey for everyone. Remember progress is not always in a straight line.

To begin this process of self-examination—of digging deep—I always start by asking clients to send me two lists. The first: ten things you're great at mentally, both on and off the golf course. The second list: ten things you need to improve. The framing is important. It's positive. These aren't ten things at which you're bad. They're ten elements that need work. This process can spark a curiosity about what you do well and what you need to work on, and that can lead to clarity about what needs to get better and how to get there.

The lists can be all over the place. "I need to work on course management. I could be better at letting go of a bad shot. Instead of seeing the trouble to the left, I need to focus on hitting my target." Stuff we all deal with when we play golf—and stuff so many of us deal with in our professional or personal lives: "I have to balance my responsibilities better. I have to improve on letting go of a poor decision or a bad day. I need to concentrate on the positive outcome I'm pursuing rather than obsessing over the things that went wrong. I need to be better at leaving work at the office so I can be present with my family." It's not terribly hard to come up with lists of your own. Try it.

Thus begins the examination of your golf game. Or your life. Or both. This process involves a high level of self-awareness, of being truthful with yourself. That's who it's most important to start being truthful with. Not your playing partners. Not your friends. Not your coworkers. Not even your spouse. Yourself. When you start being truthful with yourself then you can do that with others. What do I *really* need to work on? What am I really holding back? What am I numbing out with three drinks a night? What do I *not* want to feel or learn about myself? Is there something from my past—a troubled relationship with a parent, abusive behavior from an old coach—that is still holding me back years later?

There is a vulnerability that's required in all of this. Take Justin Thomas, who I began working with in early 2023 and who has talked publicly about our work. A two-time major winner who reached the No. 1 ranking in the world, Justin struggled with his game later that year. He didn't win a tournament. He didn't make the PGA Tour's playoffs. He missed the cut at three of the four major championships and finished tied for 65th in the other. He felt lost.

But through all this, Justin was committed to growing. Behind the scenes, he was working *extremely* hard on his mental game. Privately, he showed curiosity about what led to his slide and wanted to put in the effort to fix it. Publicly, he showed vulnerability.

"It's what Julie kept hammering into me: 'It's going to end. You're not going to always continue to play so bad,'" he told NBC early in 2024. " . . . You know, we're men, and we're just supposed to push things away, and if you actually have or express feelings, you're soft. And sure, to an extent, I definitely think there's some stuff that you can toughen up and handle. But there's others that, over a handful of years, if you just push stuff down and you haven't really gotten it out and talked about it, then it can wear on you so much more than you think."

That's pretty raw. Justin is clearly curious about how his life experiences relate to his golf game. He's committed to growing through being vulnerable and self-aware. So he's willing to mine whatever needs to be mined to get where he wants to go. Pull up the backhoe, and start digging.

Why is vulnerability important in digging deep? Because only if we're vulnerable—only if we're open to taking responsibility for our actions—can we honestly assess ourselves. Just as Justin says in assessing what men—particularly male athletes—have been taught, talking openly about feelings can take a measure of courage. Brené Brown, an academic and author who has spent decades exploring the human condition, says: "Vulnerability is defined as uncertainty, risk and emotional exposure. Can you name one act of courage that you've ever been involved in or that you ever witnessed that did not involve uncertainty, risk and emotional exposure? And it's a loaded question, because I know the answer is 'no' because I've asked it thousands and thousands of times."

In professional golf—indeed, in all sorts of professions— the idea of becoming vulnerable with the goal of digging deep can be met with resistance. I once had representatives for a prominent player approach me and say, "In ten words, tell us why we should hire you." My response was even more economical: "Because my clients and I dig deep," I told them. A couple of days later, they came back and said about their client, "He's never going to do that." That's fine. He should hire strictly a performance coach, someone who deals with execution of the golf shot rather than the whole person. I'm not knocking those people. They just do different work from me.

Say a performance coach finds that you're a procrastinator. They might give you ten tools to deal with procrastination. This could sound cheesy or far-fetched, but what if there was a reason way back in your past that caused procrastination that had a deeper meaning or a greater consequence, and you never look at that? I do think those ten tools could turn into Band-Aids. Not always. But more often than not. And when you're digging deep, you're not covering up issues with Band-Aids. You're doing the surgery that can be more painful, but has a better chance of healing the wound.

Traditionally, sports psychology has taken a cognitive approach. Lots of performance coaches help people become less scared of challenges by turning them into opportunities. They help change anxiety into excitement. They use language to help frame emotions in a more positive light. It's a rational approach that helps reshape sports—and the skills that go into them—in ways that make them more approachable, more manageable, and less intimidating. It's effective, and I don't want to criticize it. Indeed, my work takes advantage of all the above, and it's an important step in getting a golfer—or a basketball player, or an executive—to transform from someone who's put off by challenges into someone who owns them.

But I would argue that all of the work you put into reframing how you see obstacles and adversity is influenced and colored by what you bring to every situation from your past. That could be your relationship with your parents and your siblings. It's how you view yourself, your own sense of self-worth. It includes your insecurities, what you overcompensate for, what you're confident about, and what you might be ashamed of down deep. Unless you bring the entirety of who you are—your emotional foundation and all the experiences through the years—using the language and the intellectual approach to help change how you view challenges will only be partially effective. It's part of the process. But my approach is that if the process ends there, we haven't put in all the work. In order to accomplish greatness—and then sustain it—we need a more complete, holistic approach.

In psychology, we talk about someone being *defended*. A defended person often has built up such a wall around them that they don't even realize they're putting up a wall. There is an absence of self-awareness. They take no responsibility for their behavior. Frequently as practitioners in the mental health field, if we come across somebody who's very defended, we often consider not taking the case because we know we might not get very far unless they are willing to dig deep.

This is important because defended characters can come up when we look into our past to try to figure out the cause for present-day behavior or tendencies. I see this all the time on the PGA Tour. One player I have worked with felt enor-

11

mous pressure to perform from his father. (Well, actually that's *lots* of players I have worked with, but let's just use this one example.) When the player hit an errant shot, the father would yell and put his head in his hands. If the player bogeyed, the dad would throw a tantrum. It was completely stressing the player out.

Because it's important to treat the whole person—not just the golfer, but the whole person—we decided I should talk to the father. Here, though, was a perfect example of a defended person. He took no responsibility for anything he created—unless it was positive. If his son was bothered by his father's behavior, the son wasn't tough enough. If his son couldn't perform with his father on site, it was because the kid was weak.

The effects on the player's performance were enormous. But here's what's important: The player had to be vulnerable enough to admit that his father's behavior was strangling him. That vulnerability led to the courage to tell his father, "I can't handle you at my tournaments. This is important to me. I have to put up some boundaries, and until I work through this, I need to draw a line: Please stay away from the tournaments."

There is risk, uncertainty, and emotional exposure in this approach. What's also true: Digging deep here helped the player realize that he needed to understand what was triggering him and have the courage to act on it. As important as taking responsibility for your own actions, choices, and behavior is understanding what you're *not* responsible for. (In this case, his father's reactions.) This doesn't have to be finger-pointing, but rather surfacing the true reasons behind struggles or negative emotions.

Any fundamental change requires making decisions. It requires taking responsibility for what one creates in their own life. Why am I working so much? Well, that's my decision. Why do I not exercise more? Why do I not take care of myself? Why do I drink too much? Why can't I stay in a relationship?

The only person who's going to be able to answer any or all of those questions is yourself. And the way to answer is to take responsibility. Take responsibility for the mistakes, but also take responsibility for creating successes and wins and being the best version of yourself. It can't just be about the mistakes and the flaws. It has to be about your successes too. Having a positive mindset is a choice. Taking responsibility is a choice.

That's for a professional athlete. That's for a 2 handicap who really wants to push herself to the next level. That's for a 20 handicap who wants to chop shots off his index. That's for the executive who wants to better project herself at meetings. Any and all have to be honest about how they talk and treat themselves. They have to frankly assess whether they're rushing to the first tee, whether they're looking at their phones when they arrive there, whether they're curious about the best ways to get better and stay committed to their own growth.

• • •

When Wyndham Clark was in that 18th fairway at Los Angeles Country Club, I knifed through the crowd and made my way greenside with the rest of his team—his brother and sister, his agent, his girlfriend, and some other friends. The week had played out perfectly. Wyndham's golf was brilliant. His mind was strong. He wanted me there for his warm-up sessions on the range and for his practice rounds. We talked about everything—everything except golf.

And before each round, we would walk from the range to the first tee. Just before he went under the ropes, I'd ask him, "Now, what are your goals?" Setting goals—for a round, for a season, for whatever challenge we face—is an important part of drawing out your best performance, and we'll get into specifics later in the book. In the final round, Wyndham was paired with Rickie Fowler, a longtime fan favorite, in the last group of the day. Like Wyndham, Rickie was looking for his first major championship. Unlike Wyndham, Rickie had been in the spotlight for years. He had won The Players Championship, the PGA Tour's flagship tournament. In 2014, he finished in the top five of all four majors. He had twelve top-ten finishes in majors. Wyndham had only played in six majors, and never finished higher than 75th. By no fault of Wyndham's, the crowd was going to be on Rickie's side.

So one of Wyndham's goals on that Sunday: Whenever he heard "Go, Rickie!" or "Come on, Rickie!," he simply deflected it and said to himself, "I got this," and remembered his own goals. It was a way for him to take the crowd's energy for his opponent and channel it into his own game. It was a way for him to stay focused not on what Rickie was doing, but on what he needed to do.

"It was great walking by, hearing a lot of people chant for Rickie's name because it fueled the fire underneath me that I could do it," Wyndham said after the round. "My mental coach, Julie, told me . . . 'Every time you hear someone chant, "Rickie," think of your goals and get cocky and go show them who you are.' I did that. It was like a hundred-plus times today, I reminded myself of my goals."

From the 18th fairway, he just needed two more good shots to make the par that would win him the U.S. Open. The first was an 8-iron approach from the middle of the fairway. We had a perfect view. We knew the iron shot was on target. But from our angle, we couldn't tell whether it would reach the pin. When it settled at the front of the green, maybe 50 feet short, the energy palpably rose. Our entire group— which included my husband and, for the first time at a major in one of these situations, my two adult children—kind of squeezed and huddled together. An incredible mix of tension and excitement enveloped us.

When Wyndham finally nestled that long putt near the hole and had just a couple of feet left to win a major championship, we knew. I felt so much joy for Wyndham and thought about our quick journey, from a phone call in December to a meeting in February to a breakthrough first victory on the PGA Tour—to this. At that moment, I looked across the green at John Ellis, his caddie. John had encouraged Wyndham to talk to me in the first place. John had been there for the peaks and valleys, for the moments of rage and the sense of unrealized potential. I watched as his entire torso contorted, his shoulders raised up and down with joy and relief. I could see years of stress melting off of him.

When the final putt hit the bottom of the cup, Wyndham and John embraced, and all the experiences from the past melted into that hug. I waited in line on the green behind what seemed an endless array of people who wanted to congratulate the new champion. Finally, officials were going to take Wyndham to the scoring tent; he had to sign his scorecard for the victory to be official. Before he strode off, I said, "Wyndham. Wyndham!" He turned around. We hugged. And he just started bawling. A little while later, when I walked into the post-tournament party, the crowd started chanting, "MVP! MVP!" The group tried to get me to drink champagne from the massive U.S. Open trophy. I couldn't lift it, and it spilled all over me. What an amazing moment in my career.

We can all do some version of what Wyndham Clark did in that final round of the U.S. Open. Sustaining that state of being is another challenge. But at any point in our lives, we can all set goals, put them into action, and positively affect how we play and how we live. I have watched this work with dozens of players—stars who have won the most prestigious tournaments in golf, lesser-known characters who simply wanted to improve, college golfers looking to find their way, and everyone in between. This book should provide some lessons that you can put into play on the course and off of it. But start with the most important one: If you really, really want to get better, you have to figure out what makes you tick—consciously and unconsciously. You must take that Socrates quote to heart, because an *examined* life is absolutely worth living. Get out the backhoe, and let's dig. Deep.

Chapter 2

# My Story

*"Until you make the unconscious conscious,*
*it will direct your life and you will call it fate."*
—Carl Jung

"Dysfunctional" is kind of a popular word. People throw it around pretty casually these days. My work environment is dysfunctional. My family life is dysfunctional. My relationships are dysfunctional. We say it about all sorts of situations. It's overused, to be honest.

I grew up in a dysfunctional environment. It was dysfunctional in complicated ways.

My mother extolled the virtues of holistic medicine; she was actually a trained naturopathic doctor. She would say things that she was convinced were healthy but were not conventional wisdom. Don't stand in front of the microwave. Definitely don't warm anything up in it that's wrapped in plastic. Actually, just get rid of the microwave altogether. She believed that electromagnetic waves from cell phones could damage your brain. She sold a small metal button that would stick on a phone to make it "safer."

"This is good science," she would often say. To support

her cause, she would leave out magazines that listed small studies from Sweden that supported her point of view. She told us never to cook with canola oil, because once it was heated, it contained toxins that were carcinogenic. (That later turned out to be true.) She used a special microscope to look at your blood and see things she believed modern medicine couldn't identify. Molds, parasites, viruses—everyone's blood told a story, and my mom had herbs and vitamins to fix every malady. She had small brown bottles with tops that screwed off and would precisely measure the exact amount of liquid that would eventually cure me—or anyone else she was trying to help. I wasn't sure if she knew something I didn't, something the medical world had neglected to consider. I was also sure she was a bit off. She would make me take a tablespoon of cod liver oil instead of the Froot Loops my childhood friends had for breakfast. She was convinced these series of facts were essential to one's health.

My mother was—and I don't say this lightly—also mentally unstable. She was diagnosed with clinical depression. She would numb those feelings by drinking three martinis at night. That excessive drinking would lead to flirting with *my* boyfriends. She would stay out late partying, and I would have to check to see whether she returned home after a long night. It was difficult to square her beliefs in holistic health with her obvious sabotaging of her mental and physical health through alcohol abuse. My childhood felt emotionally and physically unstable. In so many ways, I had to raise myself. I received very little guidance, and basically grew up as a street kid who had to scuffle along to stay fed and dry.

# MY STORY

My father was only part of my life for six years. He was a trained social worker. My parents, older brother, and I lived in suburban Detroit. My parents had a volatile relationship. My dad was initially diagnosed as clinically depressed as well. He was repeatedly institutionalized after several attempts to kill himself. Eventually, he was diagnosed with schizophrenia. He lived with demons that he couldn't shake. He underwent shock therapy. He was prescribed medications. None of it worked.

On Halloween night when I was six years old, after one last release from an institution, my father went to my bedroom and finally succeeded in taking his own life.

Obviously, this was devastating. But one of the hardest parts about my father's absence was being left with my mother as a solo parent and guardian. Following my father's death, many different men paraded in and out of our lives. I so hoped one of them would stick, and I'd have a role model. I dreamed that having two parents would finally make me feel safe and that everything would be okay. My mother finally married one of these men. I tried to embrace him and my new stepbrothers and stepsisters, desperate to find a new, stable family. It was hardly smooth, but it was better than being alone with her.

That marriage eventually collapsed. When it did, my mother packed up our Volvo station wagon and did the hippie thing—moving me and my older brother from Michigan to San Francisco.

As a young girl, this move changed my world in so many ways. I tried to adjust to my new school and friends. Our

19

blue shingled house in Northern California was enveloped by a canopy of redwood trees that smelled so different from the oaks and maples I had known in the Midwest. There were no more cold nights, no piles of snow, just cool mornings and warm days, then unrelenting weeks of rain. The kids felt different, the school buses looked different, and I actually started to like my new life.

I also started to believe that my mother had somehow done something good for me, that the move would help. We could start over, and being in northern California in the '70s could even be exactly what the doctor ordered. I was never sure of her motivation, whether it was for me or for herself. But it didn't matter. I started to live my new life. I just couldn't shake the nightmares.

I started having nightmares when I was ten years old—before we moved out west. I would dream that redwood trees were falling on my house. There were no redwoods in suburban Detroit. I'd never seen one. To her great credit, my mother started me in therapy when we were living in Michigan. Back then, a young girl talking to a therapist wasn't typical—or so I thought. But this doctor—I'll never forget, Dr. Zamorsky—not only started to help me with my nightmares. He taught me how to go somewhere else in my mind.

Even now, teaching a kid this kind of skill might not be recommended. Somehow, Dr. Zamorsky felt like I could handle it. He would encourage me to talk in detail about my nightmares. He would have me listen to meditations. He taught me to visualize positive things happening and encouraged me to learn about myself. In different situations—

whether things got scary at home, or if I had to concentrate on the spelling bee at school—he taught me how to put my mind in the most serene place so I learned how to be aware of what I was feeling, *feel* what I was feeling, and shift to a healthier place of self-awareness. I didn't know it then, but I was learning to dig deep.

Dr. Zamorsky was totally different from my mother; an adult who was stable and a trained professional whose beliefs and teachings were rooted in his academic background. He was calm and measured in how he spoke to me and a wise, influential guide who cared for me. He listened patiently and helped me to explore topics I could never talk about with my mother. I finally had a healthy parental figure I could trust. I could start to see how my mom was a single mother who was just doing the best she could in difficult circumstances. But I realized I had to learn how to save myself. Dr. Zamorsky helped me to feel safer and look at the world as a place in which I could learn, thrive, and find my way. He made what felt impossible somehow seem possible.

My work is about my clients' journeys, and this book hopefully helps apply those experiences to the journeys we all undertake. It's written and designed to transfer some of these lessons I've learned and studied to all of you. I tell my story because I think it's important to know that my work and the subsequent guidance I provide in this book are rooted in something very real and very deep for me. I know how much digging deep into my own life experience has contributed to my career choice—the lessons provided here aren't just learned from a book or a class. They are lived.

As I mentioned earlier, my mother drank a lot. She also used drugs. After we attended dinner with her friends, she often was unable to drive. One night in Santa Cruz, I had to drive us down a dark winding mountain road, and had to sit on propped-up jackets just to see the road. I didn't yet have my driver's license. I knew it was not normal, but it was *my* normal. I always had to read the situation, identify when she was too inebriated to drive, then take responsibility for her safety and mine, finding another way down that winding dirt road in her Toyota Celica. This was my personal journey and the deck of cards I was dealt. Because of this, I not only learned how to grow from obstacles and adversity. I learned how to turn them into courage.

As my early years became a little more manageable, I was able to attend school and adjust to my new life. When we first arrived in the Bay Area, my mother enrolled me in public school. I transferred to the elite Marin Country Day School for eighth grade, and then enrolled in the Urban School, a private high school in San Francisco. My grandmother paid the tuition, because my mother's addictions made it impossible to bring in a regular income. I continued my work with a new therapist who helped to reinforce the lessons of trusting myself, and learning to be resilient to the many challenges my mother would create. I learned to understand my situation and live my life, keenly listening for ways to find safety and to understand any possible threats to my world. In those days, if a child lost a parent at a young age, they could receive social security checks. I found out later in my life that my mother forged my signature and stole these checks—money intended for me. My mother also kept money that my father had left for me before he took his life and used it to pay our living expenses.

I always felt during these times that I was different, that no one had the troubles I did. I often felt embarrassed about my home life and didn't want friends to come over. My best girlfriend, Jennifer, remembers to this day that when she would come over to my house I wasn't allowed to play or hang out until I had cleaned the toilets and done the dishes. My friend was shocked. She lived in a world where she had daily chores, but there was an adult to help. With my mother so often sleeping off a bout of drinking, I was the caretaker in my own home.

I had to be constantly vigilant growing up, always the adult in the room. If I lapsed, if I let down my guard, bad things could and did happen. I learned to simultaneously be a daughter and a mother to my mother. The roles were blurred, and it was difficult. But those were years of paying attention to small details, of learning to anticipate people's moods, learning to almost read people's minds. (When my own kids were in high school, they would comment about how I could read minds— which isn't great when you're trying to get away with normal high school stuff.) I had learned to be razor-sharp and hyper-aware of my surroundings, studying how external reality was a mirror of our internal reality—a topic I became fascinated with later in life. I became interested in applying my experiences to a career. I became interested in helping people and connecting them to their inner world. I wanted to help those committed to living a life of self-awareness and digging deep.

I'm sure these experiences—both the mundane and the traumatic—had a profound impact on not only who I am, but what I do. Because my upbringing was rooted in chaos, I can empathize with people who have had similar childhoods. I wanted to learn how their pasts might be affecting their futures. I learned resilience in order to survive, and I can help others learn to leverage their own skills.

After I completed my master's degree, I met my future husband. We moved to New York City, and I began a counseling practice. I announced to everyone I knew that I had begun to work in the psychology field. Referrals started trickling in. I came to love the work. It was liberating to help others see things inside themselves rather than always being in my own head. I've always been a good listener, but now I was being paid for it. I discovered New York and loved the energy and intensity of so many people I met.

After a year of my counseling practice, I started to attract high-profile clients. My husband would always be shocked. "You know he's currently starring on Broadway!" But I never really cared about my clients' fame. Emotions are emotions. People are people. There was no limit to who would walk through my door—actors and actresses, singers, authors— even a few professional athletes. People were comfortable talking with me. It didn't matter if they were famous or at the top of their field. The work and conversations about life, grief, pain, and growth fascinated me. It's clear to me now that this interest could all be traced back to my own sessions with Dr. Zamorsky and the therapists who followed him.

We eventually left New York with our little toddler and

moved to the suburbs outside Washington, D.C. A couple of years later, I pursued my doctorate. I became very interested in sports and decided to choose a path that merged the ideas of healing, hard work, and challenging oneself as a path to success. At the time, there were zero graduate programs in sports psychology. It wasn't a widely known or accepted field.

I took courses that had anything to do with goal-setting, or learning about anxiety. I focused my studies on mental strategies related to competition and performance. I learned clinical techniques and studied research on performance. I learned to trust my intuition. I had an instinct for seeing into the world of people's thoughts and emotions. I recognized patterns that were holding them back, and I loved working with people to attain their lifelong dreams.

Gabor Maté, a well-known psychoanalyst, has written beautiful things about trauma. He speaks of understanding one's own relationship to trauma and managing the impact on us. The bind of the trauma loses its hold on a person when we start to identify the hurt and the memories and forge a different relationship to those events. We can learn to create our own identity and self-worth through making a new connection to our past and not being controlled by how we reacted to events long ago. It isn't the trauma that persists, but our relationship with that trauma that can continue to bind us if we don't take the opportunity to examine our past.

A year into my doctorate program, an old college friend introduced me to a PGA Tour player who was having a challenging time in his marriage. He was seeking counseling. The couple began flying to Washington to talk with me. I didn't know that much about golf, but I was convinced I could learn as much as I needed to know to apply to this couple's counseling. The player liked how I worked with them as a couple. Their relationship improved. And guess what: He started playing better golf.

A year later, the player invited me out to a tournament, a regular tour stop in the Midwest. He realized that if he liked how we talked through the issues with his marriage, he might respond well to how we could talk through on-course issues as well. This was 1998. I had no familiarity with any of the rhythms and routines of professional golfers, of a tournament, of any of it. We went for a practice round. I met a few more players. And that weekend . . .

. . . He won.

My client's tournament victory didn't necessarily happen because he and I had been talking. It wasn't because we had worked to fix his marriage. Remember: This isn't a straight-line, linear process. This was a fluke. He had the talent. He had the game. He had won before—even a major championship in his past. He would win again. The player, though, believed there was a relationship between our chats and his performance. This guy believed in the work. He wanted to keep going, so I committed to work with him for a year.

I found a way to use my survival skills and intuition to create something positive, rather than avoid something negative. I could help others to live their dreams and excel in their lives. I was hooked. I started to delve into the players' performances, the ways they were feeling, the issues they dealt with. I watched sporting events. I became fascinated with coaches and their methods. I learned about athletes' motivations, their goals, their habits, their personalities. I couldn't get enough. I read books on tennis, archery, fencing—whatever I could find. I was obsessed with learning how athletes discovered an edge and what made them succeed. I had found my passion and was committed to helping others.

Through all that, I came to believe something I still believe today: We're all dealing with the same issues. That includes professional athletes or businesspeople working in Silicon Valley or on Wall Street. That includes restaurant owners and recording artists. We need to see these challenges as opportunities. My clients are men and women who work so freaking hard at their profession—at their craft—but can become so sad or frustrated when they're between the ropes or on the court or the field. Their self-belief can go down or their confidence can dip—if they even had confidence in the first place. Maybe they're haunted by negative thoughts. Maybe they're not mentally tough enough. That's no different from how any of us might feel in a profession we have thrust ourselves into. Their earlier trauma—big or little, major or minor—could be buried and reflected in their sport or their career. I loved finding the shovel and digging it out.

That first golf client introduced me to other tour players. Before long, I was working with another player, this one in the top 20 in the world rankings. That led me to a top-10 player, and within a year, I was working with tour players who were close to winning their first major and believed our work would help them attain their goals. These guys were competing for the biggest prizes in the sport. They were players with the talent and the intent to become No. 1 in the world.

A few years ago, the brother of one of my clients killed himself on Thanksgiving night. My client was in the middle of her successful career with major tour wins over a five-year period. She struggled with the memories of her brother, and how angry she was that he had taken his own life.

After her brother's death, the player couldn't bring herself to compete for a few months. She was so sad to lose him, but much angrier and more traumatized at the way he took his life and the trauma he left to her and her sisters to heal. She lost all confidence and interest in competing. The thrill was gone. She started to develop small nagging injuries. Once she returned to tournament play, she became depressed and started missing cuts. She was furious after poor shots and couldn't concentrate on the course. She was often frustrated and irritable when we met and only began talking with me because her husband begged her to get help. She did not want to speak to anyone. "What do they know? I've read books. I know about this stuff. What is anyone going to tell me? They don't understand what I've been through. No one can understand me. There's no point in talking."

I listened patiently and understood her frustration. Obviously, I have my own history with a relative's suicide. So many of us have experienced something similar. We know it's lonely to suffer in a situation where you truly believe no one else can understand. The process of growth in my work starts with focusing my attention and caring on the place where people hurt. At first, my client was barely able to talk about her brother's suicide. The mere act of *trying* to remember it created anxiety. She was having panic attacks two or three times a week. She could no longer get on airplanes and didn't want to go to any tournaments that required flying. She was stuck—and she wasn't particularly hopeful her circumstances could change. She met with me to get some relief from her emotional pain and repair the trauma, but she really felt like it would torment her for the rest of her life.

We worked slowly to build trust between the two of us. We worked together to look at photos and videos of her brother for one minute at a time. With each viewing, she became less anxious. She started to realize that the real trauma was her relationship to the memories of what happened and not the actual event. She realized she could change her response to the pain and the experience. Session after session she started to feel better. Her mood improved. She started to practice again. She started playing rounds with friends. Eventually, she worked up the courage to enter tournaments. We worked diligently to close out the negative thinking and feelings. While competing, we worked to put virtual blinders on—just like a racehorse—that would limit her internal and external distractions. Guess what? She won her first event back!

That's a specific story, but it's surprising how often similar situations arise. How have the most difficult experiences in your life impacted you? How have you overcome them? What do you still have to work on to get past them? In my experience, many of my athletes and people from other professions have endured some sort of trauma as they strive to be champions. Maybe not with the full-on dysfunction in which I grew up, or the tragedy my client experienced, but traumas along the way that can simultaneously be small, but meaningful. Some people call them big T's and little t's. It might be the trauma of losing someone in their life, a move, their parents' divorce, the failure to make a team—whatever. Yet these experiences can help us to learn about who we are—if we are willing to look. This can often bring a greater sense of self and autonomy. I have always felt that the past trauma in my life made me comfortable relating to the struggle of my clients.

In this book, there will be numerous references to different professional athletes, mostly golfers but also players from the NBA, the NFL, and MLB. Most of the stories will remain anonymous because I have a simple policy: I don't talk about (or in this case, write about) my clients unless the client has spoken about our work publicly. I have changed some of the stories slightly to protect the confidentiality of those I work with. Plenty of them are comfortable with our work and want their fans to know their experience. Others aren't. Either approach is fine.

Readers who are golf fans might know a few of the clients who have either allowed me to work with them in public or talked about how I might have helped—Justin Thomas, Wyndham Clark, Max Homa, and Phil Mickelson among them. The caution comes here: In the stories I tell that reference an anonymous golfer, be careful about trying to guess who it might be. Over the course of a quarter of a century,

I have worked with prominent players—major champions, Ryder Cup heroes, people who reached the top five in the world rankings—who have never felt comfortable revealing that we worked together.

That reluctance to go public gets to a stigma that remains about taking care of our mental health, which I'll address later in the book. Mental health care is a personal matter, and if some clients want to keep our discussions and strategies private, it's my obligation to do so. Therefore, there are tales in this book from the PGA Tour. But it could not be subtitled "Tales *from* the PGA Tour." These stories are written not to spread gossip. They're written to help.

I began this work more than twenty-five years ago, and there was a great stigma about seeking help. That original nickname of "Stealth" came because I always worked out of the limelight. Back then, I was seldom on the course doing public, in-person chats. In fact, my clients and I often worked with so much discretion that it morphed into secrecy. I once had to meet a player in a hotel, and he insisted on taking the freight elevator to avoid detection. Some clients would occasionally wear hats and sunglasses when we met in public so they didn't draw attention. Fortunately, acknowledging the importance of mental health has grown more widely accepted. My younger players will often discuss our work on social media or in their interviews. The integration of mental health into sports has been a key change in my work and I am hopeful that seeking mental health help will eventually be seen as no different from working with a physical trainer. It is a commitment to your health. Period.

My approach is learning how to process what was really going on with a person by working with them one-on-one and learning about their emotional world. All of this became clear when I began working with golfers and other kinds of athletes. These lessons I have learned—and in turn, impart to others—may start from working with PGA Tour players, but they extend to anyone who is trying to grow and live their dreams. This book is for people trying to improve on and off the golf course, to understand their past so they can improve their present, whether they experienced dysfunction that shaped them or are just trying to live their best, fullest life.

All of us know people who manage to thrive despite lives of chaos. Wouldn't you choose to live a life in which you understood your wounds and don't just put bandages where you hurt? That's the goal. Let's get to work.

# Chapter 3

# Observe, Don't Judge

*"A bad attitude is worse than a bad swing."*
—Payne Stewart

Playing golf isn't akin to performing brain surgery. Sure, maybe it can feel as difficult. But we'd all agree—whether at your own club or in the U.S. Open—the stakes just aren't as high.

Think about how a brain surgeon—or an astronaut, or a first responder, or anyone in a high-stress, high-performance environment—must conduct herself. They must stay focused on the task at hand. They can't afford to constantly evaluate how well they're doing their job. The task right in front of them is too important. If the brain surgeon's mind is busy worrying about whether the scar she creates is going to be ugly, she is not staying present while she makes the incision. If a first responder is caught up in whether a victim finds her tone of voice rude, she isn't focused on observing their symptoms. If a CEO is thinking about whether or not people respect her while she's speaking, she isn't concentrating on the words coming out of her mouth. Don't get me wrong: It's important to evaluate your technique. But you can't do it while you're trying to execute or compete. Most importantly, you can't allow the evaluation of your technique to turn into self-judgment. Your technique is not who you are.

Professional golfers get wrapped up in their play. They're on the 15th hole, but they're thinking about the short putt they just missed on the 14th. They're on the final hole of a tournament with victory within reach, but their minds are stuck on what their family and peers might think if they can't close it out and take home the winner's check. Their self-judgment distracts them, just like it can distract the brain surgeon or the first responder. They attach their scores to who they are. Their finishes serve as tangible statistics that can morph into their entire identities. Their judgments fester. At worst, they can affect the way they treat their families and handle their relationships—including with themselves. Does a player conduct himself the same way at home when he wins versus when he misses the cut? It's hard, because their performance—and their results—are there for everyone to see. They become defining.

And let's be clear: this kind of performance anxiety doesn't just live at the highest levels of competition. It's experienced by amateur golfers, graduate students, single mothers, people in all sorts of professions and all stages of development. Even kids who are learning the game. A fourteen-year-old might hit a bad shot and feel like he's disappointed his coach, his parents, and himself all at once. The pressure doesn't magically go away with age. If anything, it morphs into something worse. Emotional mastery isn't automatic. It's learned, and it requires a lot of unlearning of the ways we deal with stress. It takes work. It takes intentionality.

There's a simple thought I share with my clients all the time: "Observe, don't judge." The path to self-judgment is so easy to wander down. It's so important that we don't allow ourselves to amble that way. Only if we learn to observe our behavior and our actions from a neutral space—rather than judging ourselves—can we truly be present in our work and in our greater lives. Shifting attention to internal thoughts and away from a central task doesn't yield optimal performance. A commitment must be intentional, devoid of external or internal distractions. It's harder to make a 15-foot putt for par when you're thinking about a disagreement at work or at home earlier in the day. Recreational sports can be our sanctuary. We should use that time to have a singular focus on bringing our best effort forward. There is certainly a time to evaluate our execution and performance. That time just isn't when we're between the ropes.

I want to make a distinction between self-*judgment* and self-*evaluation*. There's often a time for self-evaluation or even what we call self-critique. That's best during practice or lessons, when we're working on our game but not concerned with the result. But in my opinion, there is rarely a time for self-judgment. You just missed a five-foot putt. That's not the time to evaluate whether you lifted your head or misread the green. Nor is it a time to declare, "I'm a crappy putter" or assess that this is the biggest weakness in your game. The timing of those evaluations is crucial. Objective assessment of your technique should come on the range or the putting green, not in the middle of competition. During competition, if a moment comes up that feels technically off, make a note and stow it away. Deal with it after the competition is over.

This concept can apply to all of us—including myself. Those of us who are working parents can almost certainly identify with the feeling of being spread too thin. We feel like we're doing everything at a B-minus level. If we get to an "A" professionally, we fall into a "C-minus" at home. We spend time with our kids and think, "I should be working on that project." We spend time with our clients and end up at, "Oh my god, I'm neglecting my family." The requirements of a professional golfer's job are set entirely by the individual player. There's normally no team practices or team travel or team meal schedule to abide by that provides some measure of structure and balance. A golfer's schedule—including how much time to devote to work and how much to spend at home—is up to each player. Because of that, spending time on the range instead of with the kids can feel like a choice. And so many of them can judge themselves for choosing one over the other.

It's important that in seeking that balance—in evaluating how we're doing at golf or at work or in life—we are observing what is happening, not judging it. There's a difference, and it's distinct.

Observing, for me, is way more neutral than judging. Notice what you did, what the result was, how you carry yourself after, how you respond to what happened. "Oh, I pulled my drive left, and it took a hard, unlucky bounce into a bunker, and now I have a difficult shot. Darn." Or, "Hmmm. I led that meeting by trying to motivate my team by setting lofty sales goals. They didn't react very enthusiastically." Or even, "I was still so upset about missing that last short putt that I wasn't in a good headspace when I hit the next drive."

Judging has a negative association. It can lead to nonproductive emotions and easily spiral out of control. "Why did I pull my drive left—*again*? Ugh, I'm such an idiot. Then I get screwed with a bad bounce and have to play an impossible shot over the lip of that bunker? I'll be lucky to make a double bogey." Or, "Man, I blew that presentation. There's no way the team can meet those goals—and they know it, and they know I'm foolish for setting them. But how can I pull that back now?" Judging ourselves can allow situations to get away from us quickly.

After a poor shot, you might be analyzing the mechanics of your swing and trying to remember and feel the sensation of hitting the ball properly. Balancing the need to understand why the ball went left and anchoring yourself in a positive mindset for the next shot is the goal. Learning and analysis can be done quickly—but only if you're observing what you did, not berating yourself for it. The next step is resetting for the next shot, getting back to the place where you trust your swing, where you remember what that best swing feels like.

If you've ever spoken to yourself in a judgmental way (and I promise you have, because we all have), you know how crippling it can be to your sense of self-worth. It's so easy to lose perspective and lean into black-and-white thinking: I'm bad, my opponent is good, etc. It can make you feel powerless. Whether you're an elite golfer or a bus driver, everyone has to deal with the weight of making mistakes. They're inevitable. They're what makes us human. We must forgive ourselves and keep moving forward.

And by the way, forgiveness in this context doesn't mean excusing poor behavior or pretending mistakes didn't happen. It simply means allowing yourself the space to acknowledge the misstep without creating a narrative of personal failure around it. You missed the shot. You stumbled through the speech. You forgot to pick up your kid's prescription. That doesn't make you bad. What we're striving toward is the ability to say, "That happened. Now what do I do to overcome and move forward from the mistake?" Consistently being able to observe our failures without beating ourselves up about them can be a superpower.

There's a famous quote from the musician Randy Armstrong: "Worrying doesn't take away tomorrow's troubles. It takes away today's peace." In my opinion, judging does exactly the same thing. And if we're taking away today's peace by judging what we're doing or how we're performing, our next steps—our next shot—won't be originating from a good place.

This isn't just a philosophical or emotional concern—it's biological. When the brain is under stress or in a self-critical mode, we activate the amygdala—the small part of the brain that helps process emotions. Activating the amygdala triggers the body's fight-or-flight system. This stress response narrows our cognitive function and inhibits our ability to creatively problem-solve or perform physical tasks with finesse and precision. If your hands are trembling with self-directed rage or anxiety, how can you expect to hit a soft chip shot or have a calm, connective conversation with your child? Observation without judgment activates a different part of the brain—the prefrontal cortex—where logical thinking and mindfulness live. When we judge ourselves harshly, especially in repeated or habitual ways, we reinforce neural pathways that associate our performance with threat. The brain begins to interpret mistakes not as opportunities for learning but as dangers to avoid—essentially confusing personal growth with personal survival. This can lead to chronic stress, anxiety, and a reduced ability to regulate emotions.

Studies in affective neuroscience—the study of how the brain processes emotions—have shown that self-criticism is associated with increased activity in the default mode network (DMN), the brain's system for self-referential thinking, which becomes hyperactive during rumination. On the flip side, self-compassion and nonjudgmental awareness correlate with activation in areas like the anterior cingulate cortex and insula—regions associated with emotional regulation, empathy, and resilience. So practicing observation without judgment isn't just a nice idea; it's a neurologically supported way to optimize your brain for clarity, composure, and performance. I work with a player who is prone to fits of anger. In fact, I work with many players who are prone to anger. Throwing clubs or cursing on the tee are ways to express frustration and anger. Holding anger will just cause persistent neurological and chemical pathways to circle and lead to a negative state. Learning to accept your mistakes and both forgive your judgment that you should have done better and let go of the negative energy is key in recovering from the mistake and preparing for the next shot.

Judging ourselves can take all sorts of forms. "I'm not taking care of myself." "I'm not eating right." "I should exercise more." "I'm not focused enough on my work." "I should be able to lower my handicap, but I can't." Part of observing, not judging, is allowing ourselves a little grace. Are there time constraints that have prevented you from working out? Can we think about what's next rather than what's past, and order a salad for lunch instead of a burger? Are there reasons why it's understandable that it has been difficult to perform at work? Are there external factors out of our control that have impacted outcomes professionally? What we want to form— by observing, not judging—is more of an opinion with altitude, highly attuned to what's happening and why, rather than devolving into self-criticism.

Think about the best coaches or mentors you've ever known. Did they berate you? Or did they analyze what happened, provide feedback, and encourage you to try again? Be that kind of coach for yourself. Be firm and honest. But above all, be kind. If you allow grace to enter your world, then you're better able to trust you can overcome your mistake or setback.

It sounds fairly easy. Why, then, is the default mode so often to judge ourselves rather than just observing and moving on? I think that's one of the million-dollar questions, and it's why I spend so much time with my clients who need their brains to be rewired in order to achieve an observational state. If you're a fan of professional golf, you can probably think of the players who best deal with bad swings or bad breaks. I'm not going to compare my clients in that regard, and I'm not going to speculate about players I have only watched dealing with those misfortunes but haven't talked through their processes. But it wouldn't be surprising if some of the best players in the world are the best at getting their minds back to neutral when the inevitable negative developments arise. We all know successful people who have anger management issues. We know coaches or parents who employ a "tough love" approach. That might work, but it's not my choice to build long-term success.

In meditation—which we'll get into later in the book—we struggle to *not* think. Trying to not think, after all, is ultimately thinking. Instead of resisting thought, you simply label the thought without judgment and move on. "My arm feels itchy." Note it as feeling. "How long has it been already, am I done yet?" Note it as impatience. "Ugh, I can't seem to make my mind empty!" Note it as self-criticism. The whole point is that the noticing is not meant to be interpretive. You note the thought as simply as you can and without judgment, so you can get back to being present. It's the act of having the self-awareness that you are in the future or the past and once again bringing yourself back, even if you do it a hundred times in a 10-minute sitting.

Mindfulness is the act of attending to oneself and noticing how you're feeling without judgments. It frees us to choose our response to any particular stimuli. We choose to live an intentional life supported by our awareness of ourselves and our environment. We choose our responses, rather than losing control over what is triggered by a negative feeling. It's not what happened to you, but how you *respond* to what happened to you. That's an important theme that will come up time and time again.

I talk about this with players all the time. Hit a lousy shot? Make a poor decision? Notice what you might have done. Take 5 seconds, or 30 seconds, or a minute and observe what happened. Was it technical? Were you tight? Was it this? Was it that? After a bad round, sometimes I'll literally say, "Okay, you've got five minutes to beat yourself up, if that's what you need to do." Then, it's over.

There's an astronaut named Mike Massimino who has adopted what he calls "The Thirty-Second Rule" for people in his profession, where mistakes must be acknowledged and overcome quickly before they're exacerbated and a situation becomes dangerous. But Massimino believes "The Thirty-Second Rule" is applicable in all sorts of situations.

"When you make a mistake, give yourself thirty seconds of regret," Massimino wrote. "Take a timeout. Feel miserable. Berate yourself. Beat yourself up. Say all the horrible things to yourself that you want to say—only, you know, do it silently in your head so you don't scare the people sitting next to you.

"Because regret is natural. Disappointment is natural. It isn't healthy to suppress those feelings or deny they exist. You need to let yourself have them. But keep it to thirty seconds. Then it really is time to move on. After your thirty-second rant, let it go. Leave the regret in the past because it will not help you in the future."

That's true in space—and on the golf course. I think it's incredibly important that we acknowledge our disappointments and missteps and mistakes, yet it's all about timing. Acknowledge that you're pissed off that you missed that three-foot uphill putt with no break in it. You don't have to write a whole novella about it. Acknowledge it—and *then* move on. Just take time to say to yourself, "Okay, that happened." Then turn back to the present, to the next task. In coming chapters, we'll look at what tools we can equip ourselves with to return to that state.

But even within that permitted period of self-flagellation, there can't be judgment. Being honest with oneself is crucial. But if we're our own judge, we also need to be our own cheerleader in order to heal the wounds. A constant environment of self-judgment can spread into someone's entire life—their friendships and professional relationships. That's the opposite of leaving work at the office (or golf at the course). It can be counterproductive. Judging can bring a burden to the pursuit at hand. What we're seeking is something completely different, what I like to call "burden-free golf."

Self-judgment is a burden, for sure, because if you're judging yourself, your shots, your pace of play, your mindset, a million different things—it can lead to being extremely pissed off at yourself. That's a burden. When you don't let that burden go, it can affect your entire round—or, really, your whole day or your whole life.

Another burden is comparing. One of the most toxic forms of judgment is measuring your own worth against someone else's. Or for that matter, someone else's performance. This is especially tempting in golf, where your playing partner's score is right in front of you on the same card. "Why did she hit that fairway and I didn't?" "How come he never seems to chunk a chip?" Yet, the truth is: comparison robs us of presence. It forces us out of the moment and into self-doubt. And usually, we compare their best with our worst. Instead of asking, "Why can't I be like them?," try asking, "What can I learn from them or from myself?" That subtle shift turns envy into curiosity.

Think about what else could be a burden. Are you arriving at the first tee late or thinking about a meeting you have the next day or a to-do list of chores at home? Are you actually scheduling a business call during the round? Are you allowing yourself the time to play golf free of distractions, or is the golf a distraction from a long list of items you feel like you should be tending to?

Burdens, too, can arrive externally, only to have us internalize them. I was giving a talk at a country club near my home in suburban Washington. The audience was invited to submit questions, and one person asked something particularly interesting: "What if I have a playing partner who just won't stop talking about things other than our round of golf?" This partner was talking about buying her couch, about redecorating her home, about going shopping, her latest haircut or exercise routine, or even about plans for the weekend—all the while not keeping up with a proper pace of play, and not really paying attention to the match at hand.

Here's where observing—but not judging—and playing burden-free golf merge. Anyone knows how annoying we might find that kind of playing partner. Pick from a long list of irksome habits—talks too much, plays too slowly, is inconsiderate of others in the group, doesn't know proper etiquette, blows cigar smoke everywhere. Those are all behaviors coming from the outside. But if you allow them into your own head, who are they hurting other than yourself? You're allowing external behaviors to become your burden.

One solution: Observe the behaviors of others, but don't judge them—just as we want to observe our own mistakes but not crush ourselves for them. In ourselves and others, acknowledge that they're annoying you. Note it. But then instead of getting wrapped up in judging, think of a potential solution. It's kind of like a normal life skill, right? If someone's rude to you at the coffee shop, it can be hard to shake. You can walk out of there fuming about it or decide to acknowledge what happened from a more neutral space and move on. You can imagine what the rude person's day was like and find empathy or humor in their response. Simply noting someone's rude behavior could even be a reminder for you to bring kindness forward that day.

This happens on the highway. Some driver is all over the place, going way too fast, cutting you off and nearly causing an accident. That can be scary, and it's a reason for anger. But in my opinion, if you carry that anger while they're off at 90 miles per hour and are way ahead of you, who's that really hurting? Yes, judging the situation could lead to a productive response: I don't feel safe enough in my Mini Cooper, and I need to evaluate what I'm driving, because that was frightening. But in general, carrying that judgment and anger is a negative spin. It's very similar to how we want to deal with a bad golf shot or a lousy hole: Observe that the guy was driving like a maniac, acknowledge that it made you feel unsafe and angry, but understand that the healthiest way to get back to a neutral state is to prevent yourself from fuming about the situation all the way home.

On the PGA Tour, there's all kinds of gamesmanship that goes on within groups. Just like at your club or in your regular game at the public course, one guy enjoys playing with another more than he does a third. That can be because of differences in pace of play. It can also be because an opponent is known for standing in a certain way—too close, perhaps, or maybe just within peripheral vision. The reaction can become a burden: This guy's a jerk, and he's really ticking me off. Who wins in that situation? If it's accidental, he's annoyed you. If it's intentional, he's accomplished his goal. He might get you saying, "We're coming up to another green. He's going to stand just on the edge of my line of sight again." If you're judging all of that, the burden can be real: The opponent can change your internal state, and even your blood pressure and your muscle tension. You're no longer neutral. You're agitated. It's time to have self-awareness and time to find a comfortable place inside yourself. Nothing on the outside can touch you when you are in your self-induced cocoon.

About being neutral: It's actually positive. When I talk with clients about getting to a neutral place, it means accessing a non-excited state and being very present. That old sports cliché—"Don't get too high or too low"—applies.

That's the entire goal. Suffering is a big word, and I don't use it lightly. But suffering comes when you can't get your mind to neutral. If you can't be present, if you can't rid yourself of burdens, you're more at risk of suffering. Suffering happens in the past, when you're still beating yourself up over that double bogey. Suffering happens in the future, when you're thinking about the par 5 that's ahead and you need birdie to make the cut. Your mind can start to race. Buddhists say that suffering is caused by resistance to reality. But if you're present in this moment—and now in this moment, and now in this next moment, and continually on and on—then you're not suffering. Remember you can practice this at home. Just like hitting shots on the range, mental strategies can be ingrained by working at them wherever it's convenient.

I had a client who played a lot of video games. On some level, they're very competitive and exciting: If you don't kill the bad guy, then you don't get to the next stage. But quite often, the people who play them are very engaged and focused. They're not holding on to the anger if somebody shoots them because the stakes are low, and if you lose the game at hand, there's always another game to play. My video-game-enthusiast client liked to describe his optimal level of focus and calm on the golf course as somewhere between a seven and nine—exactly the range he was when he was playing video games. Content, engaged, focused, quiet, present, and able to execute. That's neutral. Neutrality can be hard to envision. There is a calm place in the moving river or under the ocean waves where the environment is still. There can be stillness despite constant motion. The Sufi poet Rumi said,

"Life, like a stream of water, is renewed and renewed. . . . Though it wears the appearance of continuity in form."

Meditation is about striving to find a neutral state. The stakes are low there, too. All we're meant to focus on is one breath at a time. Inhale, exhale. Try it right now. Repeat that. We'll get into meditation in more detail, but even with a few mindful breaths, it's easy to see how you can already get more neutral, right?

So what are some concrete ways I can take this lesson into my life? Let's review:

- **Observe your behavior:** Whether in your meditation practice or while you're driving your kids to school—whatever you're doing—when you find yourself doing negative self-talk, note it. For extra credit, keep a tally of how many times this happens a day. Notice how when you start to label it, it loses its power.
- **Use the 30-second—or 5-minute—rule:** If you find yourself being negative about a performance or an outcome, allow yourself a certain amount of time to be upset. It should be defined, with a finite ending. After that, move on to the next task.
- **Allow yourself grace:** Remember that you're out here just doing your best. You can't learn without making mistakes. Embrace them as a natural part of growth. Give yourself grace.

Back to our golfer who was upset about her playing partner who was blathering on and on. We can be reluctant to confront people in these situations. Either we know them, and we don't want to upset a friendship, or we don't know them at all, and we don't want to come off as a jerk. To deal with this, I made up a concept: This woman shouldn't *con*front them. She should *care*front them. What would *care*frontationally talking to this woman feel like? Well, you might say, "You know, I just love this game so much, and the time on the course is so valuable and uplifting to me. I really like to take this time to focus on my game and pay attention to what I'm doing. Sometimes I hear you talking, and that breaks my concentration. Maybe you could walk off the green a little more if you're having a conversation and I'm putting? I'd really appreciate that."

With that, go back to the present. Take deep breaths, look at the nature around you, note the discomfort, and bring yourself back to whatever you're doing in that moment. You got yourself back to neutral. You're back to playing burden-free golf. And when something goes awry, you're far more prepared to observe without judgment. That's a simple thought you can carry with you on the course when shots go awry or your performance lets you down: Observe, don't judge.

## Chapter 4

# Tools

*"It's not about the number of hours you practice. It's about the number of hours your mind is present during the practice."*
—Kobe Bryant

Early in the 2025 PGA Tour season, I was walking the course following a client in the final round of a tournament. We were near the driving range, and all of a sudden, I heard this incredibly loud, smashing, crashing noise. What the heck happened?

I turned around, and a player was storming through the area. I didn't know it at the time, but the player—not a client of mine, not even a player I know—made double bogey at the 18th, and he slid down four spots on the leaderboard. That's a lot of money down the drain with just one bad swing.

The player stalked off. The sound of the crash—he had knocked down an entire wall of shelves in a fit of rage—was still kind of reverberating across the range. A minute later, his caddie walked by. I didn't even know the guy, but he said quietly as he passed, "My God, does he need to talk to you."

For most of us, getting angry on the golf course is inevitable. Hopefully not knock-over-a-wall-of-shelves mad, but upset by a poor shot or a bad break or the slow group in front of us. They all happen. What matters is how we deal with them. Once the shelf is knocked over—or the club is slammed into the turf, or the putter is tossed to the side of the green—there's really no turning back. You can't undo those acts, even if you consider them embarrassing immediately after. Indeed, as we have established, being upset for 5 seconds—or 30 seconds, or a bit longer—isn't the problem.

The problem is trying to get to a place mentally where those actions are prevented in the first place. Anger and frustration aren't best dealt with in the moment. If we're at our best mentally, they can be headed off before they happen. To do that, we need to create what I call a "toolbox." We then fill that toolbox with tools we can pull out and use to fix all sorts of circumstances. The tools can be for situations both big and small. Let's start small.

Say you miss a three-foot putt. (Imagine that.) It turns par into bogey or bogey into double, and it's the kind of thing we know we'll rue at the end of a round, when an 80 could have been a 79 or whatever.

Be mad in the moment. Be frustrated on the walk between the green and the next tee. Grit your teeth. Let out a roar. That stuff, in between the moments that matter, is permissible and even encouraged.

But find a tool that works for you to clear your head of the missed three-footer and move on to the next tee shot. What's done is done. What's ahead is what matters. And there's no way you can swing freely on that next shot if what's occupying the space between your ears is the missed three-footer.

# TOOLS

What is the tool that might help you move on? This is a matter of personal preference, and you might try a number of tools before you find one that works for you. I have some players who tell themselves that when their foot hits the next tee box, what's past is past and what's important is the next swing. I have others who arrive at the next shot, adjust their golf glove, and listen for the sound of the Velcro ripping away and reattaching. I was working with one of my players at the Masters, and this guy had come across the person who was responsible for making sure the tops of the trees at Augusta National looked perfect. (Yes, one guy for just the *tops* of the trees. Augusta really is a unique place.) So his tool that week became: Before he stepped into his next shot, he looked at the tops of the trees.

I have players whose driver-head cover is a caricature-like rendering of their dog. Maybe they pat the dog, and that moves them to the next shot. Some players write a word on their glove: Execute. Commit. Onward. They look at it and say it to themselves—or even out loud—before stepping over the ball. The tool can be simple. It's not important what it is. Whatever works for that particular individual.

One tool that I really believe can help in these situations— and that science supports as beneficial—is something we do all the time anyway: Breathe. Breathing, of course, is inherently unintentional, a subconscious action. We don't know we're doing it unless we think about it. We do it to stay alive.

But in situations where stress has entered our lives— situations in which, mentally, we have to get back to a more calm state—breathing can be a useful tool. There are all sorts of studies with as many or more recommendations about how to best go about this. But as Dr. Kimberly Parks, a cardiologist at Massachusetts General Hospital, said in an article published by Harvard Medical School, it's likely any type of intentional breathing practice can help—not just mentally, but even with lowering blood pressure over time. The trick is finding what's best for you.

For my clients, I often recommend something called "box breathing," which is sometimes also referred to as "square breathing." It involves a deep inhale. This is a breath that goes down to your abdomen so that the stomach extends out, a practice known as "diaphragmatic breathing." If only your chest rises, your breathing is too shallow. To make sure it's a deep breath, the stomach must move out more. One good way to know you're doing it correctly is to put one hand on your chest and the other on your belly. That way, you can feel where the deep breath is affecting your body.

For box breathing, draw in your first deep breath—the kind that moves your diaphragm—for four seconds. Then hold on to the breath for four seconds. Finally, slowly exhale through your mouth for four more seconds. Repeat that action. Repeat it again.

This can serve as a mental reset, sure. There's nothing more present—more self-aware and in-the-moment—than listening to and being conscious of your own breathing. It's calming. It's centering. It brings you right where you are, because if you're in tune with your breath and your body, there's nowhere else to go.

But breathing like that—box breathing, breathing with

intent—also affects people physiologically. It can help lower blood pressure and heart rate in the moment. It's why my clients tend to do this kind of breathing when they're getting anxious—when they're trying to make the cut, when they're trying to win, when somebody's annoying them. It might not be an every-shot thing. But it's absolutely a useful tool in pressure situations.

For those who feel better about employing a practice when it's backed up by actual data, the science behind such intentional breathing is pretty ironclad. Studies at Harvard and elsewhere have quantified the relationship between deep breathing practices and improved heart-rate variability, which can be an indication of how our body deals with stress. Heart-rate variability is generally lower in people in poorer shape and higher in those who exercise and are fit. The variations in heart rates are tiny. They can only be measured with electronic instruments. They are controlled by the autonomic nervous system, the direct line from your brain to your heart that regulates all sorts of normal functions—from heart rate to breathing to digestion.

The autonomic nervous system is divided into two large systems. First is the sympathetic nervous system, which is often described as controlling our "fight or flight" instinct—which we have learned previously is housed in a certain part of our brains. In stressful situations, the sympathetic nervous system sends blood and oxygen to your arms and legs so they can be ready to fight or run, but also takes resources from the part of the brain that helps you think clearly. Think about how that might play out when stress hits, how making sound decisions can become harder in those anxious moments. (This could be when a bear is attacking or when you're standing over a 180-yard approach shot in the 18th fairway while holding a one-shot lead.)

The other component of the autonomic nervous system is called the parasympathetic nervous system. It generally controls relaxation response. Deep breathing can help direct more blood to the part of the brain that reduces stress and encourages relaxation. It can soothe the instinct to fight or run, and reassure that everything is okay, which can in turn improve heart-rate variability. A study at Oakland University in Michigan even found that increased heart-rate variability—which generally indicates the body's ability to adjust and respond to stress—can increase our ability to forgive ourselves. If deep-breathing exercises can help our heart-rate variability, and that in turn allows us the gift of self-forgiveness—well, then, what a tool it is.

That's a lot of impact for something we might use to reset ourselves after a lousy break on the golf course. But it's also worth remembering that some of the tools we equip ourselves with don't have to be about putting behind a poor shot. They can be used to focus forward. Think back to Wyndham Clark at that U.S. Open, turning those chants of "Rick-ie! Rick-ie!" into his own fuel.

The point is that whatever tools we put in our toolbox— be they in the final round of the U.S. Open or in your Saturday Nassau—they can be used simply to make sure the mind is free and clear to execute each and every shot. We need them in every single situation we face. For now, let's stick to golf. Think about all there is to evaluate before you bring back the club. Where is there a bunker or a water hazard? What is my target? How is my lie? What impact will the wind have? Should I try to flight the ball low and run it up to the green, or is it better to bring it in high?

That's too much to think about in the midst of your backswing, a list of ingredients that—instead of making for a nice salad—would be a disaster to try to process all at once. A good tool to sort all this out and put you in position to make your best, most committed swing is to separate the tasks. The first part: Go through a routine—whatever order works for you—of everything you have to consider before drawing the club back. Lie, wind, target, etc. All of those factors need to be dealt with before you stand over the ball.

When you have all the information in your head, when you have made all your decisions, draw a line. Some of my players do this physically, taking their club as they stand behind the ball and tracing a line on the ground. Some just do it mentally. Either way, the line serves as a point of demarcation. The decision-making part of the process is over. The shot-making part of the process can begin. When you step over that line to address the ball, the only thought is about making a good, solid swing that's full of intention. It's not about the wind, because you have already dealt with that. It's not about the trouble to the left, because you are committed to hitting it right. It's not about whether to play the ball low or high, because you already decided what was best. What's left is to swing, and swing freely, and accept the result of the shot.

Those are fairly simple tools. But because my approach is to attack problems from all angles, we might want to arm ourselves with more intricate tools that allow us to dig deeper. Ultimately, we're trying to rewire our brains to perform tasks and create habits that become more natural, more hard-wired. That might take a different form than just listening for the Velcro on your golf glove or patting your doggy head cover.

There is a practice called neuro-linguistic programming (NLP) that gained popularity in the 1970s through the book *The Structure of Magic* by Richard Bandler and John Grinder. To be honest, it's kind of out there—what I like to refer to as having a "woo-woo" quality. It's somewhat amazing pseudoscience that can seem far-fetched as it connects the brain and its processes to language and acquired behavioral patterns. It could make some people roll their eyes. But after studying it years ago, I actually carried some of it into my work. NLP includes tools that I find to be useful.

Take one: There's a process in NLP in which a mental coach or therapist and a client go through a process that's somewhere between a meditation and actual hypnosis. Together, you're trying to access a great feeling from your past.

Go back to Wyndham Clark at that 2023 U.S. Open. In Friday's second round at the par-5 14th hole, he tried to carry a 3-wood to the green for his second shot. Instead, the ball floated short and left of the green, settling in some thick rough. When he got to the ball, Wyndham knew he would have to take a full swing with a wedge to loft it out of the gnarly grass and onto the green. He did just that, flying the ball high in the air before it settled softly onto the green, setting up his birdie putt.

"He went for the hero shot and he pulled it off," one of the NBC announcers said. Then he rolled in the putt. "Should Wyndham Clark go on to win the U.S. Open championship, undoubtedly he'll look back at 14, that up-and-down, for a birdie."

And he does. That feeling of pulling off that shot, of making that birdie, is exhilarating. How can we access feelings like that again? In NLP, we might literally close our eyes and think about the environment in that moment. What did the air feel like? How strong was the breeze? What were the clouds like? See the buildings. See the galleries. See the green. See the pin. Remember every detail we can.

Then, think about the shot. Get to the point where we are reliving that swing, that moment, the one that felt so good and was executed perfectly. In NLP, they use something called an "anchor." That might be, as you're allowing that sense of place to wash over you—right as you're feeling the most elation, the best emotion—taking your index finger and touching it to your thumb. The idea is that, in the future, touching your index finger to your thumb will bring that feeling roaring back. It's almost Pavlovian.

I realize that seems pretty out there. But NLP practitioners have worked with military veterans who have endured trauma, with first responders and all sorts of people who have seen horrific things. And they really believe that they can summon the best, most palpable, most elevating emotions by transporting your mind to the past, then using a physical trigger to access those feelings.

The point is that there are many paths to positivity. Go back to that PGA Tour player who knocked over the shelf because he was so frustrated he made double bogey on the 18th. The truth is, such manifestations of anger aren't uncommon on tour—or, frankly, at the club or the muni on Saturday morning. But what if we could retrain our minds to access positivity even when we're frustrated or upset?

A question I get all the time, both from PGA pros and amateurs: What if I can't stand the person or people I'm playing with? This can happen on tour, where the groups are selected by officials. And it can happen on a regular weekend round if we don't have a full foursome and someone else fills in. Chemistry and camaraderie are traits that make golf special and fun. When they're interrupted—or outright hijacked—it can be unsettling, or worse.

The annoying partner—whether he smokes too many cigars or talks too much, like the lady in the previous chapter—is a problem. But it can be dealt with by looking at it as an opportunity to focus on your own game. If you're playing with someone obnoxious, why get caught up in their obnoxiousness? Instead, lock in on your lane. Use a tool or a trigger to make sure you're not concentrating on what Rodney Dangerfield is doing, and that you're only concerned about your game.

Slow play can be difficult in this regard. That's true on tour, where if one player in a threesome is slogging his way through a round, all three players get put on the clock—and are threatened with a penalty. But that's true for all of us, too, because we become obsessed with how long a partner is taking over a shot or to find a ball, concerned that the group behind us is waiting too long, freaking out that we're losing touch with the group ahead of us. We're generally becoming miserable.

What's the tool to access here? One way to combat a partner's slow play is to control your own walking. Breathe. Take in the outdoors around you. Disconnect yourself from what your playing partner is doing, and instead embrace what *you're* doing. Find a rhythm—a slow rhythm—to stride and think. There's no point in racing to your ball if you're only going to have to wait ten minutes to hit it. A mentor of mine called these "stackers"—behaviors that are opportunities for us to learn and grow in situations that might seem averse to anything like that. Divorce yourself from blaming the partner and acknowledge that we don't know what people are going through. The slow-playing partner might be like that maniac who cuts you off on the highway. The instinct is for anger. The reality should be for empathy. Who knows what's going on? Let's create a stacker, and build upon our experiences positively even when it seems difficult, by arming ourselves with tools that allow us the ability to access our best selves.

That's not always easy. Let's take one of my players. At one tournament, he hit a poor shot. Actually, it couldn't have been *one* poor shot. Something was building in him. He turned to his caddie immediately and said, "You fuck up every hole." He was having so much anger come up, and it wasn't the kind that lasted five seconds or a few minutes. It was affecting his golf game and his life.

Now, I'm sure I can name some golfers—or basketball players, or high-level athletes or performers from any number of pursuits—who play great when they're angry. For a time, they find a way to fuel the emotion in the right direction. "I'll show them," or, "You shouldn't have done that to me." I have talked to players who have said, "I'm at my best when I'm ticked off." If that's the case, we don't want to take that emotion out of them. (As long as it doesn't involve knocking things over.) Again, these are individual strategies for individual people. There's no one-size-fits-all remedy.

But I don't think playing angry is a great long-term strategy. Not for your golf. And not for your life.

The good thing about my player in this instance: He knew he was angry. He was aware his emotions were negatively impacting him and those around him. And he was seeking tools to help deal with it all. That goes back to curiosity. That goes back to self-awareness. That goes back to being willing to grow. That goes back to an examined life being well worth living. Only then can we figure out what's causing the anger, what was causing him to blame someone else for his own mistakes.

Moving forward, though, he needed tools. Tools that helped him identify the anger, acknowledge it, and replace it with a more productive and positive message. It's easier, when things are going wrong, to cast blame elsewhere—in this case, on the caddie. But did he really cause that bad shot? The trick is, when you feel that anger coming on, to flip the narrative.

Let's review a few ways we can get ourselves over a setback and return to a productive state:

- **Breathe:** Deploy "box breathing" or "square breathing" by drawing in a breath for four seconds, holding it in for four seconds, then releasing it through your mouth for four more seconds. Doing this before a round or during it can help not only your mental state, but your physical health as well.

- **Fill up your toolbox:** Figure out what tiny methods help you put behind what just happened and move on to what's next. Maybe it's feeling your foot hit the next tee box. Maybe it's listening to the scratch of the Velcro when you adjust your golf glove. Maybe it's patting your head cover or tugging your cap. Whatever works for you.

- **Draw a line:** Divide your evaluation of what's needed for a shot from the shot itself. Make all your assessments about the lie, the wind, the target, and whatever else you need to consider before you address the ball. Draw a line on the ground or in your head. Once you step over that line, the evaluations are over. All that's left is to execute.

- **Find a path to positivity:** Note what annoys you on the course or in life. Acknowledge that growing angry about it serves no one. Find empathy for others, then chart your own path forward.

We can prepare ourselves for frustrating moments and disappointing results if we take time to tend to our mental approach. Don't allow yourself to get to the point where you're storming off the course after a double bogey on 18 and knocking over a shelf in rage. That's about frustration and being furious in the moment, about the poor shots and shoddy execution that led to a terrible score. But it's also about the underlying reasons for such an outburst. In the future, it's about having the resources—and the self-awareness—to understand your behavior in the present and the ability to head it off before it happens. What a gift that would be. Start loading your toolbox with tools.

# Chapter 5

# Goals

*"Setting goals is the first step in turning*
*the invisible into the visible."*
—Tony Robbins

On a practice day leading up to the 2016 PGA Championship, Jimmy Walker asked me a curious question. Jimmy and I had been working together for a while. He had won tournaments on the PGA Tour and rose as high as tenth in the world rankings. In 2014, he finished in the top ten in three of the four majors. By this point, he was laying the groundwork for something bigger.

That day, with the last major of the year just ahead, Jimmy said casually, "What do you think of me seeing myself holding the trophy?"

It was a bold question. He had missed the cut in both the U.S. and British Opens. Winning the PGA?

I told him: "I love it. I wouldn't dwell on it. But when that thought enters your mind, embrace it. How fun is that?"

Winning a major championship is a dream so many young golfers grow up with. But leading into that PGA Championship, Jimmy Walker turned that dream into a goal.

That's not appropriate for every player at any point in time—or for any of us on the course or at work. What I knew about Jimmy at that moment: He always wanted to win a major. But he started to realize that his daily habits, built around daily goals we put into place, were now manifesting a dream. He could make a lifelong dream his immediate goal because he had put in the work to get there.

It's a really interesting and important part of my work, and it applies to all of us: What do we set as goals for a round or a day? How do we execute them? And how does that help us realize our dreams? That could be lowering our handicap into the single digits. It could be raising a model family and sending the kids to college. It could be anything in between. But we have a far greater chance of reaching our dreams if we put into place goals that help us focus and improve, but that are perhaps 90 percent attainable. I wouldn't have advised any old client to envision holding the Wanamaker Trophy awarded to the winner of the PGA Championship. That could easily be cart-before-the-horse advice. But I knew where Jimmy was with his game. More importantly, I knew where he was with his mind. He was ready.

As any of us go through this process, it's important to view various aspects of our lives from different altitudes. Our dreams are at 40,000 feet. Our goals are on the ground. We should all dream big! But we should also realize that achieving those dreams isn't likely to happen without some real foundational work first.

At some point early in the 2025 PGA Tour season, I

started something new with my clients on tour. I asked them to write mission statements for themselves.

Any executive knows what a mission statement for their company is: It identifies the organization's core purpose. It explains why the company exists. It usually outlines what the company's overall goals are. It doesn't get in the weeds on how the company executes its mission or packages its products or services. It is concise and to the point. Most important, it is grounding and foundational—words any employee can look to as a reminder of why they show up to work every day and what the outcome should be as they stack days on top of each other.

Why can't we have mission statements for ourselves? I think they can be particularly applicable to golf. They can represent a player's overall dreams about their career: They want to be No. 1 in the world. They want to win a major before they turn twenty-five. They want to win multiple tournaments. They want to enjoy each event or each round. Or they want to become a better golfer while simultaneously being a supportive and present parent and spouse.

Most of my players loved this exercise. Some of them have put their mission statements as the screen savers on their phones. Others keep them in their score book. We don't talk about them much—certainly not every day or every week. But they serve as an anchor for each of them. Whether they're in the heat of competition in a tournament or they're home with their families, the mission statements serve as a reminder of why they're doing all this in the first place. They help articulate their big-picture goals—so big-picture that they could be labeled dreams—and, in moments of stress, can help them take a deep breath. If today is just one step toward living out our own mission statements, it can take the intensity or the fear of failure or disappointment away from a given situation. Having the mission statement as a pillar in the background can help make a missed putt or a poor round feel less frustrating.

Another area in which a mission statement can help is when we create a false narrative about what is happening in our lives and why. We have to be careful with how we spin things in our own heads. "Oh, my ball took a weird bounce out of bounds; I always get screwed." Or, "My boss doesn't value my work; she never gives me credit."

I had a client who advanced to the Tour Championship in August one year, the final leg of the FedEx Cup playoffs in which only the top thirty players qualify. By this point in the season—with all four majors over, with the season-long fight for money and status concluding—players can be grouchy. My client was that, and worse. The final tournament is always in Atlanta, so the complaints are easy to predict: "I'm hot. I'm tired. I'm sick of it. The season should be over."

Think of the narrative that player was creating for himself. There's a version of "Observe, don't judge" in assessing this situation, too. Is it hot? Sure. Is it hotter than it was two weeks ago in Memphis? Or hotter than when you practice in Florida or Arizona? Plus, what's the alternative? Failing to make the Tour Championship and not being among the elite in your profession? Who is this narrative serving, exactly? The reality is: You're right where you want to be doing exactly what you are meant to do. We should spend time and effort spinning things positively, not dragging ourselves down.

The mission statement—a reminder of your dreams—can help here, too. If we have a stated anchor that reminds us of why we do what we do, it can help control the negative narrative before it starts running away in our brains. Tired? Worn out? Beaten down by a boss who doesn't recognize and acknowledge your contributions? Having that high-altitude statement to serve as a reminder of why you do what you do can help return you to what's important. It can help lose the negative narrative that can build in our heads and remind us of the dreams we have and the positive steps we must take to attain them.

One client I have worked with over the years is Stephan Jaeger, a German who won his first PGA Tour event in 2024 after a successful stint on the minor-league Korn Ferry Tour, where he won six times. In publicly discussing our work together, Jaeger hit on the reasons to write out a mission statement—even before he had written one.

"Not everything I work on is because of the golf course, right?" Jaeger said. "That's kind of the stigma, that we golfers just work on mental stuff because we want to win tournaments.

"I wanted to be a better husband. I want to be a better father to my child. I wanted to kind of be a little more mellow. I used to get pretty angry and frustrated. I wanted to kind of start that trend in the right direction. That's what kind of started it, and it really helped with . . . golf as well.

"Now, there's a million other things that can be done for the golf course. But it didn't start because of that."

That's all a great way to think about our wildest dreams, our biggest-picture goals, our missions. Jaeger was thinking about his life from the highest altitude. We all need to be able to do that.

There's a lot that goes into that process, though, and it's not just about ourselves. It's about the choices we make about who to involve in our lives. Do those people have mission statements that align with our own? There's a great example of how those choices impacted one of my clients. This is a player who is very in touch with his emotions. During a difficult season, he had some tough breaks. He bogeyed the final two holes on Friday at one tournament to miss the cut by a single shot. At another event, marshals got distracted by an orchestrated airplane flyover just as he hit his drive on the final hole. His shot went into the deep rough by only a few yards, but because there were no volunteers who had paid attention, they weren't able to find the ball. The ensuing triple bogey was a big reason why he wasn't able to advance in the FedEx Cup playoffs.

Through all this, he was—kind of understandably— tipping too easily toward disappointment in his results, trending toward negative thoughts. That's when we reached back to consider his mission statement. He started thinking less about performance goals and more about what would make him happy—even when his results wavered or the ball bounced against him. In considering all of this, he realized he had employed both a swing coach and a caddie who weren't serving him, who actually were in direct conflict with his own reason for being. The swing coach had him thinking very technically while in competition. The caddie had off-course issues. In reengaging with his mission statement, we were able to ask, "What are you doing to yourself?"

If this player had been the CEO of a Fortune 500 company, the choices would have been obvious. If high-ranking employees were chipping away at the company's mission— if they were actively detracting from what the organization was trying to achieve—then the person in charge would have little choice but to part ways with them.

This can be harder when we're making decisions about ourselves. Emotions are involved. We're aware of other people's personal struggles. We can worry about the impact of our actions on the lives of others. But we also have to allow ourselves to be the CEO of our own lives, our own worlds.

So my client fired both his swing coach and his caddie. That kind of transaction happens all the time on the PGA Tour, of course. It doesn't mean it was easy. But you know what? The player felt *soooooo* much better. It was night and day. He hired a caddie who brought positive energy to their business. He was looking for a swing coach, but also realizing that what he needed wasn't as much technical as it was mental. What was most important: He was happier, both with his golf and with his life. What's a more important aspect of an individual mission statement than personal happiness?

"I can say very confidently the biggest difference in the good and bad days right now is my mental game and what's going on in my mind," this player told me during one subsequent tournament. "Because I was swinging very similar today and yesterday, but my process was not as clear as a whole yesterday, and I had an extremely hard time shutting off my brain versus today, when I made it basically my only goal. The number of shots I execute well when I'm clear and very minimal in what I'm thinking is incredible."

This player's decision to change the people around him was made at altitude. It was driven by his mission statement. But it also got him back grounded in his smaller, day-to-day, tournament-to-tournament goals. The mission statement might morph slightly over time as our needs change and our dreams evolve. But in general, it's a constant, a foundational piece for how we want to live and how we see our career playing out.

Goals, though, can change daily. We have talked already about the various tools we put in our toolbox, the devices we arm ourselves with in order to keep ourselves in the present and be committed to the task at hand. Goals can be extremely important tools. If we create goals at the beginning of a round of golf—or, say, at the beginning of a week of work—we can begin to put into place the habits that help build the foundation that allows us to reach our dreams. What we're doing by creating intentional, attainable goals is training the brain. It's a brick-by-brick course of action.

I love the quote from the famous motivational speaker Tony Robbins that leads off this chapter: "Setting goals is the first step in turning the invisible into the visible." That's a good way to outline that goal-setting is a part of a process, a process that can lead to realizing our dreams. There must be a commitment to the process, and we must find that process fulfilling. But the smaller goals should also remind us that we can't skip steps to get to our dreams. If we go to the gym, our goal should be to have a great workout, not to come out looking buff and ripped. The goals should be reachable, not set up to punish ourselves but rather within parameters so we can enjoy the pursuit. We set one goal to do a certain number of reps with a certain amount of weight, or to train on the elliptical machine or the stationary bike for a specific amount of time with a predetermined level of resistance. We set the next goal to return to the gym three or four times a week. We set one more goal to keep that up for a number of months. Before you know it, the invisible is turning into the visible.

I often ask my clients to play a practice round at home and keep score—not on how many strokes they take, but on how committed they are on each shot. The goal is to be engaged in all aspects of the round, and that starts with being deliberate and intentional about each element. They rate every shot on a scale from 1 to 10, 10 being the most committed. So much of what we want out of a round of golf—or while leading a meeting or giving a presentation—is to be present in the moment. Knowing you're going to rate each shot based on how engaged you are in its execution helps keep your feet where you are. The score we give to each shot shouldn't be related to where it ends up or how well we strike it; we're all going to hit bad shots. The score should be tied to whether, when we stood over the ball, we had a clear idea of what we were trying to do. Was I spacing out? Was I thinking about appointments I had later in the day? Was I worried about an upcoming commitment? If so, the score is lower. If not, give yourself a 9 or 10.

This exercise—this tool—helps reward process rather than results. We hear athletes and coaches talk about the difference between the two all the time, so much so that it can sound cliché. But understanding that process leads to results, and then putting that in play, is an important step in fulfilling our mission statements and getting closer to our dreams. It's why, when I work with players to come up with goals before a round, they're never, "Make seven birdies," or, "Shoot in the 60s," or, "Keep double bogey off the card." Those are results.

The goals should really be steps in how to deliver the results, but they're divorced from them. I'll have players decide their goal for one round is to say "LFG" before each shot. Or to walk tall with their chest out. Or to think, "Confidence," before they stand over the ball. Again, there's no one-size-fits-all approach, a theme I'll hammer home because it's so important. We tailor goals to the moment and to the player. You must set your own.

One saying I love as a goal before a round is: "Free swings to specific targets." The focus there is two-fold: The players don't want to be overly technical in the moment. Thoughts about our golf swings are best left on the range. There's absolutely a time for them. It's just not in the middle of competition. The goal of swinging freely allows our instincts and feel to take over. But we don't want to do that arbitrarily. The second part of the goal—having a specific target—helps us focus on where we're hitting it. There's an intentionality to both parts of the statement.

# GOALS

When we're at our best on the course, we're really invested in the goals we have over a specific shot or for a given day, not in the score we shoot or the place we finish. I was working with Max Homa in 2023 when he won the PGA Tour event at Torrey Pines in San Diego. Anyone who has watched Max at a tournament has seen him walk down the fairway in between shots mimicking his swing. He can get overly caught up in technical aspects of the game, just as any of us can. Technique in golf is essential. But that week at Torrey, Max explained what was important to his process in a way that could help any of us—with any type of handicap or any type of swing.

"Having a plan each day mentally," he said. "I didn't go into a single round this week thinking about a technical goal or a statistical goal. It was, 'I'm going to learn something today. I'm going to put in place what I've been working on.' And today, that's what I did. I did a great job of it."

We've talked about tools already, including the idea that we draw a line—literally or figuratively—on the ground near our ball. As we discussed, the idea is to do all the pre-shot thinking and evaluation on one side of the line, and once we step over it, we're swinging freely. A way to reframe that is something I sometimes suggest to players: Play "Think box, shot box." This can be a goal for a round: The first "box"— and it's not really a physical box, but more a space in time—is for thinking. What's the wind like? Where's my target? How might the ball come off a slope? Where's the smart miss? The next "box" is for executing the shot. It's a great way of helping organize a round of golf, and maybe it works better for you than drawing a line. You're not thinking about the score you hope to make on a specific hole. You're not worried about the putt you missed on the last. Your goal is to make all the considerations you need to on a given shot in the period of time before you address the ball. And once you address it, your mind can be clear of clutter. You can swing freely, unburdened by all the decisions that go into execution because you have already made them.

Scottie Scheffler's run through the 2024 and '25 seasons on the PGA Tour was remarkable. People can analyze the crazy stuff he does with his footwork, or marvel at how sharp he is at distance control with his irons, or talk about the improvements he has made as a putter. But what has become obvious as Scheffler talked about his approach over those seasons is how much better mentally he is than most of his competition. He said some of that focus came from the only competitive round he ever played with the player who was perhaps the toughest mentally in the history of the sport—Tiger Woods.

This was on the final day of the 2020 Masters, the one delayed until November by the coronavirus pandemic. Scheffler and Woods were paired together because they both were ten or more shots off of Dustin Johnson's lead. Woods, by that point, already had five Masters and fifteen major championships to his name. He had no shot at winning the tournament. Scheffler expected that perhaps Woods's goal for the day would be to get out of Augusta quickly and head home.

"Then we showed up on the first hole, and I was watching him read his putt, and I was like, 'Oh my gosh. This guy is *in it* right now,'" Scheffler said toward the end of the 2025 season. "That was something that I just thought about for a long time. I felt like a change I needed to make was bringing that same intensity to each round and each shot. . . .

"I don't hit the ball the furthest. The things that I do on the golf course, other people can do. I think it's just the amount of consistency and the intensity that I bring to each round of golf is not taking shots off, not taking rounds off, not taking tournaments off. When I show up at a tournament, I'm here for a purpose, and that's to compete hard, and you compete hard on every shot."

What a great way of taking a lesson from the best to ever do it and applying it to your own game. But it's also a great way of explaining that our goal when we arrive on the first tee shouldn't be to win the match or break par. It should be to employ a tool that allows us to focus on each shot. That goal before a round of golf is so much smaller than your mission statement, a tiny slice of realizing your dreams. But in order to make the invisible visible, we have to make tiny steps that turn a round that results in a score of 72—or 82, or 92, or however many shots you take—into 72 individual efforts and commitments.

Let's get to one final goal that any of us could use entering any round, be it in the club championship or a casual game with friends: Use your walk wisely.

If a round of golf takes four hours—and please, let's hope most rounds of golf take four hours or less—how much time is spent actually hitting shots? It's a minuscule percentage of the time invested for the day. There is time walking off the tee heading out to track down your drive a couple hundred yards down the fairway. There is time waiting for your playing partners to execute their shots. There is time on the green as competitors line up their putts. There is so much time.

What an opportunity. What a great goal to establish before a round. Use that time—use your walk—wisely. I like to think that, as we walk to our ball, it's as if we're carrying an old-school camera. Not an iPhone, but one of those Nikons or Canons from decades ago that needed to be focused manually. As we leave the tee box, we can give ourselves a few moments to lament a shot that went awry or celebrate the fact that we ripped one right down the middle. Either way, there should be a time limit on thinking about the shot just past before we move on to the shot that's ahead. As we get closer to the ball, we're consciously turning the lens so the task at hand—the next shot—becomes more crisply in focus.

In that way, the time between shots isn't wasted on what just happened—or even on spacing out. Sure, take time to enjoy being outside, to drink in the beauty of the course or to chat with your friends. But at some point, using your walk wisely means preparing for the next shot, maybe even getting into "Think box, shot box" mode. It's a great pre-round goal that can get us to focus on the tiny sliver of the day right in front of us—one shot to execute in a day in which dozens of shots must be executed.

And it's another example of how establishing small goals can help us reach our greatest dreams. Let's review some of the steps any of us might implement to help get there.

- **Make a mission statement:** Write down a simple sentence or two that can provide a bedrock foundation for how you live and what's important to you. This is your anchor. It could be about how you approach your golf game. More likely, it would encapsulate the guiding principles by which you want to live your life, professionally and personally.
- **Establish commitment goals:** Play a round of golf in which you rate every shot you hit not by the quality of the result but by your own engagement in the moment and the commitment to its execution. This will help train your brain to become more deliberate in your thinking about each shot—or each decision at work.
- **Think box, shot box:** Before a round of golf, make it your goal to have two separate areas of execution. Commit to doing all your evaluation and planning in the time before you step up to the ball. Once you're addressing the ball, the thinking is over, and it's time to execute the shot.
- **Use your walk wisely:** Make it a goal before a round to use the downtime between shots to your advantage. As you walk, cleanse the result of a previous hole or the last shot—whether it was good or bad—and slowly bring into focus what's next, which is all the decision-making about the next shot.

Back to Jimmy Walker at that 2016 PGA Championship, the one in which he envisioned holding the trophy even before the tournament began. That week at Baltusrol Golf Club in New Jersey was messy weather-wise. Jimmy was tied for the lead after Friday, but play was suspended early in the afternoon during Saturday's third round—before Jimmy even teed off. He was left to play 36 holes for a major championship on Sunday.

"I was just prepared, mentally prepared, to play the whole thing," he said between two grueling rounds in wet conditions.

That is what I observed. Jimmy began that week thinking about a dream of his—winning a major championship. But that dream was attainable in the present because of all the small goals he had checked off leading up to Sunday.

"I felt confident in myself," he said. "I felt confident in what I was doing, felt confident in my golf swing, my putting, my chipping. Kind of tried to wrap myself around that [idea], that everything was feeling good, and to go with that and trust what I was doing, trust all the stuff that I have been working on."

The 18th hole at Baltusrol is a par 5. Jimmy was in the final group. Just ahead, Jason Day made eagle to pull within one shot of the lead. That left Jimmy to make a par and secure his major championship. He hit his drive in the fairway. The choice then became: Go for the green in two, or lay up to a good number to hit a wedge on in three.

How did he respond? He and his caddie Andy Sanders used their walk wisely.

"I was thinking, 'You're going to make par nineteen out of twenty times—or even higher than that—from there,'" he said, meaning anywhere around the green if he went for it in two. "We're walking down there to the shot, and I'm like, 'Andy, we just send it up by the green, don't we?'

"He's like, 'Yeah, let's do it. Let's do it.'"

So they did it. Jimmy ripped a 3-wood into a greenside bunker. He dutifully hit his bunker shot safely to about 35 feet from the hole. And he executed the two-putt that gave him his par and his major championship. He didn't need to imagine holding the Wanamaker Trophy. He was holding it!

We don't need to wake up every morning thinking about attaining our dreams in the next day or week or month. But Jimmy Walker's victory at that PGA Championship shows any of us what can happen if we dutifully establish goals and then execute them. We should all dream big—as enormous as we can imagine—but simultaneously understand that realizing those dreams involves training our minds a little bit at a time. We should all make little goals that help us get there.

## Chapter 6

# Anxiety

*"I've had a lot of worries in my life,*
*most of which never happened."*
—Mark Twain

nyone who plays or watches a lot of golf knows the following phenomenon: A good player reaches the point where she or he stands over a short putt, whether it's for birdie, par, or bogey. The task is simple. They have performed it hundreds of times in the past. All that's needed is a solid, confident, committed stroke. And over and over and over again, they just can't make the ball roll into the cup. They tense up. Their knees are shaking. Their hands are quaking. Their head is spinning. They jerk the putter head through the ball. And they miss. Again and again and again.

These are the yips. They're not just in golf. There are examples from all sorts of sports. "Yips" sounds like a slang term that only golfers know. "Oh, my buddy John's got a terrible case of the yips. I feel so bad for him." It's part of the parlance of the game.

But the yips are a real condition. Look up the term in Merriam-Webster. You'll find the following:

> **yips** *(plural noun)*—a state of nervous tension affecting an athlete (such as a golfer) in the performance of a crucial action

Or, better yet, from dictionary.com, which is based on the Random House dictionary:

> **yips** *(plural noun), sports*—the sudden and unexplained loss of a motor skill used in a sport, as with a smooth golf swing reduced to a stuttering one, experienced by athletes who had previously mastered the required movements

Define it however you want. The yips are a thing. We've seen them. We know them. We may have experienced them. They're more prevalent in older golfers. They surface more frequently in competition. But they can affect players of all ages and abilities in any sort of situation.

Here's something important about the yips, though: In my work with my clients, I don't talk about them. Ever. We'll get to why shortly.

In this book, it's important to get the yips out in the open. It's also important to understand they are nothing about which to be embarrassed. What we must do is identify and discuss the root cause of the yips, something that can affect us all to varying degrees: anxiety.

We all have a visceral feel for what anxiety is and how it affects our lives. We should also know that it takes many forms. One of the most common is a diagnosable condition called "general anxiety disorder." It can vary in both seriousness and symptoms. In some cases, it can be pretty debilitating, altering and even crippling our day-to-day life. The Mayo Clinic provides a really good list of what those afflicted with general anxiety disorder can feel:

- Persistent worrying or anxiety about a number of areas that is out of proportion to the impact of the events
- Overthinking plans and solutions to all possible worst-case outcomes
- Perceiving situations and events as threatening, even when they aren't
- Difficulty handling uncertainty
- Indecisiveness and fear of making the wrong decision
- Inability to set aside or let go of a worry
- Inability to relax, feeling restless, and feeling keyed up or on edge
- Difficulty concentrating, or the feeling that your mind "goes blank"

It's obvious that general anxiety disorder can take many forms. It really can suck the joy out of life. We know we can fret about topics beyond our control. (The state of the world comes to mind.) We also know we can get mired in the minutiae that pile up in our lives. (Kid drop-off and pickup, grocery shopping, bill paying. It never ends.) Life gets more complicated, and that can wear on any of us. General anxiety disorder sends our mind into an unbalanced state in which our fears outweigh the reality of any situation. It might make us think about gun violence in a way that's not practical—evaluating whether we should go to a crowded concert or festival because we're scared of a mass shooting. It might make us reconsider flying because of the risks of a plane crash. That kind of grip on our lives is unhealthy and makes life less enjoyable. It's important to identify it and deal with it.

Anxiety doesn't have to be completely debilitating to affect performance. We can carry anxiety to the first tee. It can surface when one of my clients is trying to make a cut—and therefore determining whether they make money that week or not. It can bubble up on the back nine on Sunday, with both prestige and millions of dollars at stake—not to mention live crowds and television audiences drinking it all in. But it also can surface when we're playing a match with friends. General anxiety disorder is real, persistent, and kind of unrelenting. It's hard to control and hard to let go of, and can take some serious therapy to overcome, which we'll get to.

Performance anxiety is different. It's also real. It doesn't necessarily control your life. It just pops up in more specific situations. Which brings us back to the yips.

•　•　•

Studies have shown that there are some cases of the yips that are produced by a muscle condition called *focal dystonia*, which causes involuntary muscle twitches when a person is performing a specific task—like trying to make a short putt. But I would argue that more cases of the yips are caused by anxiety than they are a physical issue. People with the yips either have anxiety baked into their lives or have become strangled by the idea of performing. If we learn how to deal with the kind of performance anxiety that causes the yips, we can perhaps equip ourselves with tools to deal with all sorts of anxiety that can creep into our golf games—and our lives.

If you have suffered through a case of the yips, it's important to realize you're not alone. Some of the most accomplished players in the history of golf have dealt with the yips. Tommy Armour, the Scotsman who won three majors in the late 1920s and early '30s, is credited with coining the term to define the condition that eventually drove him from tournament play. Ben Hogan had a reputation as one of the best strikers of the golf ball in the history of the sport, but in his later years, he dealt with the yips to the point where he even practiced a different grip in which he separated his hands on short putts. Sam Snead, Tom Watson, Bernhard Langer, Johnny Miller, Mark O'Meara, Ernie Els, Pádraig Harrington. All won multiple major championships. All dealt, to one degree or another, with the yips.

Baseball is another sport in which prominent players have endured very public cases of the yips. Jon Lester, a three-time World Series champion and five-time all-star, had pinpoint control as a pitcher. But he infamously couldn't execute even the softest of tosses to first base to try to hold runners on. Rick Ankiel was a prized pitching prospect who the St. Louis Cardinals entrusted with important playoff assignments in the early 2000s. In one, he walked six batters and threw five wild pitches. In another, he faced ten hitters and walked five of them. He eventually was sent to the minor leagues and had to reinvent himself as an outfielder. (Ankiel's memoir is entitled: *The Phenomenon: Pressure, the Yips, and the Pitch that Changed My Life.*)

There are more. All-star second baseman Chuck Knoblauch went through a period in which he couldn't complete the simple toss from second base to first. In the 2000 playoffs with the New York Yankees, Knoblauch committed three errors in six innings before removing himself from the game. Catcher Mackey Sasser couldn't lob the ball back to his pitcher. His arm essentially stuttered as he attempted to complete the task, and the New York Mets transitioned him to first base and the outfield. Pitcher Steve Blass won the seventh game of the 1971 World Series for the Pittsburgh Pirates, but in subsequent years his case of the yips was labeled "Steve Blass Disease." He could no longer throw the ball over the plate. The yips drove him from baseball, and he became a sales representative.

Yips could affect a tennis player who can't figure out her serve. They could cripple a competitive dart thrower, whose motor skills must be finely tuned and highly repeatable. There are famous cases of the yips in the world of cricket.

So yes, the yips are real. No, you shouldn't feel bad if you have been afflicted with them. You have company. There's no shame.

But the reason I don't talk to my clients about the yips— or why I don't even use that term—is because I believe it's counterproductive. I don't like labels to begin with. When somebody starts naming what they have, the condition has a tendency to almost build on itself. Their self-diagnosis becomes a self-fulfilling prophecy, and the problem grows a mind of its own. We want to be honest with ourselves. We need to understand our actions and their consequences. It's not like you can pretend you're making your short putts when you're missing them.

Telling yourself, "I have the yips," though, could be pulling out a crutch and outsourcing your problem to a condition you know other athletes and golfers have dealt with. I've heard golfers who self-identify as having the yips, but then they don't have it on every short putt. They're able to hole a decent number—maybe a third. That's not the yips. That's inconsistency! These players might find solace in the idea that they have an identifiable condition, understandably so. Labeling the issue, though, isn't helping them fix it. I believe it's detrimental to performance. The label becomes another obstacle they must overcome. We don't need more obstacles. We need fewer!

With this kind of anxiety, there is a disruption in what we consider to be an automatic or ordinary flow of things—like how the putter is drawn back or how a pitcher is throwing to first base, actions junior golfers and Little Leaguers make all the time. This is usually a result of overthinking. The brain gets in the way, and instinct is replaced by a rush of thoughts. It can be suffocating. It feels like we might never drain our minds of all the clutter and return to a neutral state in which we're equipped to carry out a simple task. But even that's part of overthinking: If we're thinking about how simple something is, and then going right to, "But I *still* can't do it," our brains are giving our bodies no chance. Maybe you've never slipped into such a state. If so, great. If you have, join the club.

In golf, it's also important to know that this kind of repeated inability to complete what seems like an easy task—notice I've ditched the label "yips," just as you should—doesn't have to apply only to short putts. I had one client who struggled mentally with tight lies around the green. If he approached his ball and saw it was on a perfectly smooth surface—something most of us might be happy about—he would spiral downward. He just couldn't execute the shot, and he knew it before he even addressed the ball. You might have a certain circumstance in a round of golf that brings out your performance anxiety. Maybe it's trying to carry a bunker or a pond. Maybe it's facing a certain tee shot that doesn't suit your eye. Maybe it's playing from a particular distance in which you feel between clubs. We could have a group session and identify a whole slew of situations that apply.

Those times when we feel like we can't make a short putt show how performance anxiety can affect something quite narrow—the tiniest of strokes in the entire game of golf. There are larger reactions to anxiety that also come with labels—again, labels I wouldn't use with clients—and also can be dealt with if we're prepared for them. Let's talk about "choking."

Choking is a weighty concept. It's something many athletes fear. You have prepared for something your whole life. The moment arrives, and you underperform. It feels worse than any other kind of loss because it can involve an inability to execute basic skills you have put into place time and again. Ultimately, they escape you when they're needed most. That hurts. That can feel humiliating. We all know the examples. How could Greg Norman open the 1996 Masters with rounds of 63, 69, and 71 to get to 13 under par and take a 6-stroke lead into Sunday, then follow with a final-round 78 to lose by 5 to Nick Faldo? How could Jean van de Velde arrive at the 18th tee at Carnoustie needing only a double bogey to win the 1999 Open Championship, and record a triple-bogey 7 on a hole he had birdied twice in the previous rounds? He missed out on a playoff. Sadly, those are infamous collapses.

This isn't to pick on anyone. It's to make sure we don't run from the idea that allowing anxiety to take over when we're under intense pressure has happened to performers at the highest levels. It can happen to people who have prepared a great speech on paper, but when it's time to deliver it to an audience, their vocal cords tighten, and their hands shake so much they can't get a glass of water to their lips. Just as with the anxiety that affects those small motor skills we must use to make a short putt, this anxiety affects our bodies. We might have an increased heart rate, elevated blood pressure, tension in our muscles—any or all of it. If general anxiety disorder can be debilitating in everyday life, performance anxiety can be debilitating when we're supposed to execute at our highest level. Our minds are trumping our physiological aptitude. It's awful! There's no problem in admitting that.

The solutions to dealing with these issues—be they missing a series of short putts while playing golf with your buddies or failing to smoothly execute a task when you're under the most pressure—could be physical. We should probably do putting drills and make sure we have the right grip, stance, and stroke to make sure we're not missing short putts because we have a technical flaw. We should prepare for any major project by making sure we have a foundation of knowledge on the topic. We've rehearsed the speech out loud. We've studied the course we're going to play. We know what to expect.

More likely, though, the solutions to dealing with anxiety are mental—and they're not likely to come to us magically in the middle of a round. We're going to have to prepare for them. Just like when we're angry. Just like when we're rattled by an obnoxious or slow playing partner. Just like when we're upset about a bad bounce. We have to be ready for our anxiety to surface when we're not over the ball on the green, facing a short putt that can seem so, so daunting.

A big part of being prepared for anxiety is an awareness of the circumstances in which it can bubble up. As with any problem with our golf game or our work life or our relationships at home, we need to be aware of what we're feeling in order to deal with the issue. Once we're aware that we have a problem, we can address it. We all miss short putts. That's part of the game of golf. One miss doesn't mean we have a case of performance anxiety. That's one reason I don't like to label the problem, because it gives us the opportunity to invent an issue before we actually have one. But even if we're not labeling the problem, if the misses start to stack up, it's imperative that we understand how we're feeling when we're over the ball. Do our shoulders tense up? Are our arms particularly stiff? Do we move our heads?

Same with taking on those big projects or playing in a prestigious tournament. Am I nervous? If so, what am I nervous about? Are my hands shaking? If they are, what's con-tributing to that physical state?

I don't love the idea of being consumed by performance anxiety, of spending so much time on it that you almost speak it into existence. But I think it's important to ac-knowledge, when you're out of competition and away from the spotlight, that you might feel a certain way when the pressure is on. You hear about athletes trying to simulate stressful situations all the time. Football coaches pump crowd noise into practice and make their kickers try to convert field goals with the din all around them. Basket-ball coaches set up free throw drills with all kinds of dis-tractions behind the basket. Golfers hit shots pretending they're on the final hole of a major. We can imagine all sorts of scenarios in which performing might be difficult and try our best to rehearse for them.

The reality is: It's hard to re-create those tense circum-stances. A Tuesday morning practice round isn't the final hole of a major. It just isn't. It's not a waste of time to try to pretend. What's more important is that we come up with tools as we practice that we draw on when we're in the fire. (So much of this comes back to figuring out the right tools for each of us, right?) Maybe it's understanding that we're typically rigid and stiff when we address a short putt, so we develop a way to rid ourselves of that tension before we get over the ball. This could go back to breathing exercises. It could go back to creating a distraction—like looking at the trees or fidgeting with the Velcro on our golf glove. The point is to put those tools into play when we're practicing and preparing so they're naturally there to draw on when we need them. Practicing your putting? Breathe in deeply, then exhale, before you address the ball. Or shake out your arms, a reminder to loosen up. Or tug the brim of your cap. It comes back to another theme that runs through all my work: There are no wrong answers.

•   •   •

Tugging the brim of your cap might get you in the right frame of mind to address a short putt. It won't relieve general anxiety disorder. For that, we need to employ more serious tools. Meditation can help. Breathing exercises can help. But a popular and effective way of dealing with all levels of general anxiety disorder is "cognitive behavioral therapy," or CBT, which can also be called psychotherapy. I like to think CBT can help us do something that's so important when we're dealing with anxiety: flipping the switch.

Let's dig in on CBT. It can help us deal with obtrusive thinking that really doesn't make sense, thoughts that outweigh their actual importance. Let's turn to the Mayo Clinic again for a definition:

> *During CBT, you work with a mental health professional such as a psychologist or other licensed therapist in a structured way. You attend a limited number of sessions. CBT helps you become aware of thinking patterns that may be creating issues in your life. Looking at the relationship between your thoughts, feelings and behaviors*

*helps you view challenging situations more clearly and respond to them in a more effective way.*

That's all very important. We must understand that we create our own thinking patterns, which means we can control them. We have to be able to separate our thoughts from how we act so that we're not spiraling into an undesirable state. Talking through these issues can help.

Here's a good example of someone with general anxiety disorder who benefited from CBT. I had a client who had just started the drug Lexapro to deal with a mild case of depression and some anxiety issues. (Let's be honest: Drugs, prescribed appropriately by a licensed therapist, can be an important tool in dealing with anxiety. I'm not advising them as a first-option fix-all. I'm acknowledging that I have clients who benefit from various medications to help with a variety of mental health issues.) Drugs, of course, can have side effects. One potential side effect of some antidepressants is blurred vision. In extremely rare cases, they can be linked to blindness.

This woman who was new to taking an antidepressant was at a concert. The venue filled with strobe lights and lasers. The flashing and pulsing affected her vision. (Guess what? The flashing and pulsing affected *everyone's* vision.) Given that she had just started the antidepressant, and because she was dealing with general anxiety disorder, she started to think, "Oh, my god. I'm going blind."

She called me from the venue in a panic. In layman's terms, she wanted me to talk her off a ledge. In reality, we engaged in a form of cognitive behavioral therapy. She had to consciously think, "I'm not going blind." We worked through her thoughts. What's actually going on? What is the environment? Might the strobe lights be affecting her vision? We had to connect her irrational thinking to what reality was playing out before her. General anxiety disorder can cause us to default to the worst-case scenario. A gunman is a threat to this crowd. This plane could go down. Or, in this case, I'm taking a new drug, my vision is tilting off-kilter, therefore I must be going blind.

After some conversation, the woman understood. By stepping outside of the situation, she understood it better. She calmed down. I think she even enjoyed the rest of the show!

CBT can also be applied to golf. I had a client who felt like he was struggling with his game. He texted me on the Saturday morning of a tournament. He had barely made the cut. He felt he had no chance of contending over the weekend. He wrote that he was mentally struggling, that he had no motivation because his game was so lousy that it was embarrassing. He identified that he was filled with anxiety—which is a great step, the awareness we all need in such situations. But his hands were shaking. He said he hated the golf course. The situation was clearly getting away from him.

"What can I do?" he asked, the desperation coming through even in a text.

My response could be interpreted as a form of CBT. How could this player flip the switch and get back to a better mental state, a mindset that's more attached to reality? I wrote to him that the two rounds ahead were a great opportunity to work on his mental game. I didn't want him to have a technical thought or become obsessed with the physical aspects of his swing. His partner that day was set to be one of his better friends on the PGA Tour. That's a gift. Feel grateful for that. Look at the fans. Understand they're there to see you, to marvel at your game, to wish they could hit the ball like a pro—even if it was off-line. Rather than feeling embarrassed, understand that you have worked extremely hard to make the cut at a PGA Tour event and have the chance to move up the board and make some money.

"The universe is not always going to give you positive feedback," I wrote, and I believe that. "It has to come from within you. When we say, 'Enjoy the process, not the result,' this is exactly for days like these. You are bigger than your emotions. They are fleeting. You are solid."

That might fall into the "woo-woo" category we have talked about. But it's also CBT. This player was starting to spiral, and instead of spiraling, he needed to flip the switch. He could, and he did.

Think of all those negative thoughts he was having—that perhaps we all have from time to time—as clouds moving across the sky. They don't have to be stagnant or permanent. They're fleeting. We can think of them as flowing in one ear and out the other. We must realize that what we're feeling about ourselves—particularly in down moments—is not who we are. Flipping the switch is another way of saying we're changing the narrative we have created for ourselves.

Cognitive behavioral therapy can help flip that switch

and deal with anxiety. It can be helpful to have a therapist or coach begin that process. But it's also possible to talk yourself through anxiety. You can detach yourself from the narrative you've created and identify it as irrational. It's almost like summoning your inner therapist, your "Inner Julie," if you will. Feel the signs that anxiety is creeping in—an increased heart rate, tension in your muscles, whatever it might be. Then draw on the tools you have equipped yourself with to return to a physical and mental state from which you can do whatever's ahead—make the three-foot putt, deliver the presentation, sink the free throw.

Let's review a few ways to deal with anxiety that could help either with an immediate need to perform or with just getting through daily life:

- **Lose the labels:** You might feel like you have missed a bunch of short putts in a row. Don't say you have "the yips." You might feel as if you blew a match by chunking a chip on the 18th hole. Don't say you "choked." Those phenomena are real. Telling ourselves we're experiencing them does no good. In fact, labeling could create a problem where one doesn't exist.
- **Prepare for anxiety:** Understand the circumstances in which you feel pressure and how it manifests itself in your body. Practice methods of relieving tension in your muscles in situations that are out of competition or before a presentation. Be aware that you may experience performance anxiety before you're expected to perform so when the time arrives, it doesn't catch you off guard.

- **Our brains vs. our realities:** Be aware that what we're thinking might not represent what's actually happening. If you're dogged by the idea that every outcome is going to be the worst-case scenario, talk to a therapist or coach about why that isn't actually the case. Understanding how our anxieties relate to what's actually going on can help relieve them.
- **Flip the switch:** Develop means to understand that what you're feeling in a given situation isn't who you are. Be mindful when you're creating a narrative in your head and find tools that pull you back to reality. You can do this with the help of a therapist. But you can also learn to do it on your own.

In golf, we're all going to hit bad shots. Those bad shots are going to happen for all sorts of reasons. We have a flaw in our swing. The club slipped in our hands. We didn't turn our shoulders or rotate our hips. We rushed. Fill in the blank with whatever affects you the most.

What's important in minimizing those errant shots—or anchoring ourselves in our professional and personal lives—is understanding the role anxiety can play in determining how we enjoy life and how we perform. If we understand and practice for the moments when anxiety might arrive, we're better equipped to deal with it under pressure. If we're honest about how anxiety is making our brains think, we can detach ourselves from those thoughts and become more grounded in reality. It all takes work. We should embrace that, too.

Chapter 7

# Shame and Self-Belief

*"Shame corrodes the very part of us that believes
that we are capable of change."*
—Brené Brown

In the pro-am that leads up to a PGA Tour event not long ago, one of my players was paired up with a famous NFL star. That's not unusual at all. The pro-ams are typically filled with celebrities from the area, big business tycoons, or philanthropic types. The pro golfer's job in those situations is to socialize and show off a bit. A football player in one of these groups might be among the best at what he does on Sundays in the fall. But this is the golfer's stage. Let's hit some shots, make some jaws drop, and have a few laughs along the way. The amateurs are so excited to be playing golf with the professional in these events. Their outfits are often creased because they're right off the rack, special duds for a special day. They're all but giddy, anxious to show the pro their skills. The pro, on the other hand, is enjoying another day at the office—or *trying* to enjoy it, anyway.

But in this instance, I asked my client—and you might not believe this—to intentionally hook his drive off the first tee into the woods. And then, on the second tee, do it again. And on the third tee, do it again.

By the fourth hole, the NFL star and my player's other partners kind of suspected something was up. So the experiment didn't really "work." But why do it in the first place? The idea was to get the player to acknowledge that he is easily capable of feeling embarrassed by his golf game. The idea was to get him to let go of the shame so many of us feel. Maybe, if he kept purposefully hitting poor shots when he's supposed to be the best golfer in the group—by far—then he'd realize how ridiculous it is to tie his identity to whether he hits a ball in the middle of the fairway or rips it out of bounds. He's still the same person, right? By the fourth hole, he smiled as he saw his shots duck left into the woods. He was able to detach the result from his own self-worth. It was as if he was watching somebody else hit the ball. He didn't feel regret or inadequacy. He could just smile and chuckle at it all.

That's kind of a lot of weight to put into what's supposed to be a fun round in a pro-am before the player's real workweek begins. But it's a concept that's not unique to that particular player. It's both widespread in professional golf and prevalent in all sorts of segments of society. So many of us carry shame, and the way we do impacts how we view ourselves, how we handle our relationships, and whether we can muster one of the most important qualities to have and display on and off the golf course: self-belief.

To a certain extent, we can all feel exposed when playing golf. Our swing is our swing, be it textbook or disastrous or somewhere in between. The shots we hit are on display for everyone in our group. There's no hiding. That can be particularly disconcerting if we're playing with people we don't know, when we assume they're judging us based on the kinds of shots we hit or the score we shoot. Play poorly with a new foursome, embarrassment rears its head, and self-belief can drain from the body. I have players who grew up with beautiful, textbook swings that are held up as examples, and others who have swings that no one would ever teach. If the results are good, why would the fluidity of the swing matter? You'd be surprised. That shame doesn't just show up with weekend hackers. It can appear at the highest levels of the game.

Take J. B. Holmes, an accomplished player who won five times on the PGA Tour, made a Ryder Cup team, and finished as high as fourth at the Masters and third at the Open Championship. I worked with J.B. early in his career. He had a powerful swing, but it was short. People used to wonder how he could generate the length he did with such a truncated motion—and those outside assessments kind of haunted him. As a kid growing up in rural Kentucky, he didn't have the typical country club background of so many PGA Tour pros. He was smaller. He had thick hands. His swing wasn't fluid. He wore clothes that made him stand out in the field— unintentionally. His peers would mock him—at least until he launched drives into the stratosphere.

With that upbringing, J.B. had to work on the shame he carried because the other kids would make fun of him. He couldn't afford to be hurt or angered by snide comments. He had to stay quiet and just focus on the task ahead of him— the next round, the next hole, the next shot. Instead of concentrating on what he couldn't do or didn't have, he had to emphasize what he *could* do, the advantages he had over his competitors—primarily an important one, the ability to hit the ball farther and straighter than his friends! J.B. came to accept that whatever he lacked, he had a special skill that he could trust, a swing that perhaps was atypical but was certainly repeatable. What mattered: It worked. Once he was able to insulate himself from the demeaning comments from the other kids, he felt no shame about his appearance, his swing, his build—none of it.

If that kind of shame can build in someone who won on the PGA Tour, it makes sense that those of us with lousy—sorry, I'll call them "developing"—games could be vulnerable to the same problem. But here's another example of how we're all going through some version of the same thing. I'll sometimes say to my PGA Tour players, "If you were playing a round on a deserted island, and there was no shot tracer showing the shape and trajectory of your shots, no recording of your ball speed, no gallery to see where you hit it and how you played, and no social media commenting on your shots—whether they were good or bad—would anything feel the same?" The answer is uniform: No. No way. That round on a deserted island would be completely different.

That's fascinating to me. So many of the best golfers on the planet are affected by how they think they're being perceived from the outside. Take away the television viewers and the fans, the stats about how they compare to the rest of the field—their peers—and they'd immediately feel more relaxed and at ease. With no one around to judge their play, there's no shame in anything they do. When they're in their private lives at home, they walk differently. They dress differently. They sometimes *act* differently. Because they can be recognizable in public, they sometimes have a palpable tension in their faces when they're out and about.

Part of that comes with the territory. In their regular, everyday work environment, these golfers feel highly visible, even scrutinized. People watch—and judge—how they hit shots on the range. People evaluate their warm-up routines. People look at their putting drills. People know where they rank on the PGA Tour in so many categories that quantify their performance—not just driving distance, but newer evaluations like shots-gained approach that further drill down on a player's strengths and weaknesses. Even their swing speeds and shot trajectories are quantified. The result: A lot of them feel like they're not meeting others' expectations. I would say that's an extremely common issue with most, if not all, of my clients. Gambling has only increased the scrutiny they live with. The statistics can feel defining. Add the fact that people in the galleries can now have a financial stake in how well they play—and often expose the players to derision and jeers if they're struggling—and it's easy to see how their golf games and their sense of self can become so intertwined, they're almost indistinguishable from each other.

What can develop, then, is a fear of failure—or fear of what they believe *others* might perceive as failure. It's hard to hide from what could be considered failure in golf. Scorecards don't offer context. Nor do tournament finishes. If you shot 85, you shot 85. If you missed the cut, you missed the cut.

There's no ambiguity. Fearing a poor result—one that everyone can see, one against which we can't argue—can strangle the mind. That feeling is so, so common in players from all levels of golf. You start to lose your identity as a person, and you can start to reduce yourself to just a set of outcomes that are harsh and concrete. The players know that assessment is artificial. They're still John, Sara, or whoever. They're not their numbers. During tournament week, that can be very hard to remember. It sometimes takes an off-week or two to be reminded of who they actually are. (Which, of course, gets back to why we dig so deep.)

So, some of the work I do with my clients is to try to access that kind of freedom of the mind when they're surrounded by all those external forces they deal with every week. Can they play like they're on a desert island when they're at the U.S. Open? Can you play like you're alone in the evening as the sun goes down when you're in the club championship?

There's a famous quote from Theodore Roosevelt that is frequently distilled to "The Man in the Arena Quote." But it's worth considering at full length.

> It is not the critic who counts; not the man who points out how the strong man stumbles, or where the doer of deeds could have done them better. The credit belongs to the man who is actually in the arena, whose face is marred by dust and sweat and blood; who strives valiantly; who errs, who comes short again and again, because there is not effort without error and shortcoming; but who does actually strive to do the deeds; who knows great enthusi-

*asms, the great devotions; who spends himself in a wor-thy cause; who at the best knows in the end the triumph of high achievement, and who at the worst, if he fails, at least fails while daring greatly, so that his place shall never be with those cold and timid souls who neither know victory nor defeat.*

Roosevelt doesn't mention shame. But it's lurking there, underlying what he says.

What Roosevelt is arguing is what golfers or athletes—or any of us, really—should feel about ourselves: We should give ourselves credit for trying. There's vulnerability in performing in public, vulnerability in putting our games on display not on a desert island, but on television or in front of galleries or in front of the businessman who's a better player than you but with whom you've never played. That means something, and there's a certain measure of self-belief that should come from the mere act of standing up in that tee box, shoving that peg in the ground, and putting your best swing on the ball.

I've mentioned Brené Brown before, and one of her best quotes leads off this chapter. I like to give her book *Daring Greatly* to clients. Look at where the title comes from: directly from the Roosevelt quote. In a TED Talk about shame, Brown linked the two concepts—daring to be in the arena, but carrying shame with you as you enter—in a way that I think applies not only to so many professional golfers, but also to those of us who hack it around on the weekend.

"When you walk up to that arena and you put your hand

on the door and you think, 'I'm going in and I'm gonna try this,' shame is the gremlin who says, 'Uh-uh, you're not good enough. You never finished that MBA. Your wife left you,'" Brown told the audience. "'. . . I know there's things that happened to you growing up. I know you don't think that you're pretty enough or smart enough or talented enough or powerful enough. I know your dad never paid attention even when you made CFO.'

"Shame is that thing. If we can quiet it down and walk in and say, 'I'm going to do this,' we look up and the critic that we see pointing and laughing—99 percent of the time is who? Us. Shame drives two big tapes: *Never good enough*. And if you can talk it out of that one: *Who do you think you are*?"

That's a lot to digest, particularly when applied to a round of golf. But it gets to how deeply rooted shame can be—for all of us. There is no difference between my player starting a tournament and a writer trying to put the first words on a page. What do I know? Who am I to tell anyone about something? Or a singer whose job is to belt out the highest note in front of ten thousand people—all of whom are, at some level, assessing the performance. Shame is a potent emotion often linked to higher rates of both anxiety and depression and low self-esteem. Shame in athletes has been studied more recently, and those studies have revealed a need for interventions related to self-compassion. We need to have empathy for ourselves and for others rather than harshly judging our performances. We have to prac-tice understanding. One study—not surprisingly—showed that the development of self-compassion—which can be displayed by less self-criticism—is related to better performance in sports.

Part of my work is identifying not only which clients are carrying shame, but what the source of that shame is. You might see a high-level player react angrily to bad shots—even slamming or throwing a club. A famous example would be my client Wyndham Clark at the 2025 PGA Championship. Frustrated by a bad drive in the midst of a bad round, Wyndham hurled his driver. In cases like that, what we're trying to figure out is the root of that anger. If it's simply bad golf, well, fine. Work on that. But so frequently the embarrassment associated with poor play can come from our pasts. There's a direct link between shame and trauma. It's quite common on the PGA Tour to have trauma based in childhood, and for that childhood trauma to be linked directly to the expectations and behavior of a coach or a parent.

I know so many high-level players whose fathers were more than just demanding. They were borderline abusive. Some of them were narcissists. Some of them had personality disorders and were driven to make sure their sons accomplished goals they never reached themselves. The father of one of my players used to ride in a mobile wheelchair and follow his son on the course as he played. He would speak to his son throughout the round, voicing his praise or disdain depending on the result of a certain hole or shot. If the rules hadn't disallowed it, he absolutely would have given his son swing advice in the middle of a round. The entire fiasco finally unraveled when the father's scooter toppled over on a slope by a green. Play stopped. Marshals righted the wheelchair and propped him back up. It was a scene. Imagine how composed his son was on that subsequent putt!

That player was clearly scarred by his father's behavior. So as we dig deep in trying to bring out the best golf in my players—or in an executive, or a parent, or whoever—it's important to acknowledge there are pieces of our upbringing that inform our present, and to get at what those might be and what their impact continues to be. Brené Brown lists some of those possibilities: a parent didn't acknowledge our accomplishments; an academic pursuit was left incomplete; we were told we just weren't good enough, so we believed it then, and we believe it to this day.

Examples are everywhere. If any of us have carried shame through our lives, we should take some solace in the fact that we're not alone—not close. I have another client who had a coach growing up who told him something along the lines of, "You're so talented, one of the most gifted students I've ever had. You could get to be a top-ten player in the world. Not number one. You're not that good. But top ten for sure."

The player became a successful pro, and he never felt like he dwelled on that assessment. But as we were digging into whatever was holding him back—from not winning a major, or not reaching number one in the world—we did some deep meditation. He mentioned that old evaluation from a long-ago coach. Now, I won't say whether this player had the capability of being the world's top-ranked player. But he definitely identified the years-old assessment as something he carried, even though he didn't realize it. He allowed another person to place limits on what he could accomplish. And he was ashamed. It took repeated digging at his own limiting beliefs to explore his memory and get him to understand he was still carrying it around.

I have also had players who are extremely self-deprecating. That quality can seem admirable—an ability to laugh at yourself, remain humble, understand that you're not as good as people might build you up to be. Self-deprecating comments about your own golf game can be hysterical. But I also think self-deprecation can be a mask behind which some players hide. Are they putting themselves down to deflect attention and elicit a chuckle? Or are they putting themselves down because, deep down, they really don't believe in themselves? So often it's the latter, and it's something we have to work on—getting rid of that shame to discover, or *re*-discover, your self-belief.

That deep-down struggle with self-belief can show up on a particular shot or in a particular tournament. But there's also a part of the struggle that can hang over an entire career. Even at the highest levels of golf—or maybe *especially* at the highest levels of golf—I have found that so many players have what we would refer to as "impostor syndrome." Are they really as good as everybody thinks they are? If they're ranked tenth in the world, are there really only nine golfers who are better than them? Over the years, I have had a lot of clients who wonder if their confidence is real or deserved. Or, somehow, have they fooled everyone?

That can go back to shame. Of the dozens and dozens of players I have worked with, those who dealt with a difficult upbringing—trauma from an aggressive and demanding father, for instance, that led to a lot of shame—tend to have impostor syndrome. Shame actually causes harm to the body, and is associated with increases in cortisol and inflammation, which is not good for us. There are numerous reports about the linkages between post-traumatic stress and shame, and how they cause persistent distress and psychic dysfunction. I have come to believe there's a pretty direct relationship between the two. If you were told at a young age that you weren't good enough, that you'd never amount to anything, how couldn't you carry that with you into adulthood, even if there was plenty of evidence that you belonged on the PGA Tour—or as the CFO of a Fortune 500 company?

I'm not immune from it. I've been working on the PGA Tour and with professional athletes for more than a quarter of a century. But I still have moments when I wonder, "Who am I to be helping a professional athlete perform at their best?" I'm no expert on the golf swing. I don't know the proper form to shoot a jumper. There are times when my players are struggling, and I can't divorce myself from their results and wonder about the quality of my work. Am I failing them, and therefore they're failing? My self-belief wavers, and I have to remind myself: I have been doing this a long time. My heart is fully invested in the work. I'm doing the best I can, and my skill set—over time—has shown it can truly help people perform.

And I can relate to how easily one can feel judged. I was playing golf in Florida, and one of my clients was practicing at the same course. Now, I don't put in the practice work to improve my game very much, and I don't play often enough to be consistent. Why would I care what I looked like? I should just go and have fun, understanding the limits I have placed on myself. But in this instance, I told my client, "You're not allowed to look." Is that vanity? Maybe. The client, of course, snuck a peek anyway. He made a tongue-in-cheek comment on my swing. And I still felt ashamed. I felt he was judging me. But whether that was true or not, I actually was judging myself. Note to self: Practice what you preach.

Shame—and sometimes, the resulting impostor syndrome—can also be built from within, from our own standards. So many golfers who achieve something great wonder whether they deserved to do so in the first place. There are major champions who wonder whether they *won* a certain tournament, or another person *lost* it. There are players who run off a string of high finishes, maybe even snagging a win or two, and when their game goes away, they struggle with whether their hot streak was really because of the work they put in and the talent they have or if they just got flat lucky. The record shows they posted those results. The checks all cleared, and they're left wondering: Was that a fluke? Am I really that good?

The way to work on impostor syndrome is to change the mindset. That comes from digging in on any false belief and shame that we're carrying—where it comes from, why it looms over us all these years later. This can take time and effort. I was dealing with a new client who had won multiple times on the PGA Tour and risen into the top 75 in the world rankings by his mid-twenties. But his game deserted him.

He started missing cuts. He fell below 400th in the world rankings. He had to go back to the Korn Ferry Tour, the top minor-league feeder to the big leagues. When the lousy results began piling up, he started to say, "I'm just going to walk away." There are times when this game can be extraordinarily discouraging, right?

I became convinced that this player was ashamed that he could no longer play the way he once did. He thought he just lost his swing. But there's a chicken-and-egg element at work here: Is he losing his swing, and then becomes embarrassed and feels terrible? Or is he embarrassed that he can't play like his old self, and therefore his swing deserts him?

Either way, changing the mindset involves rebuilding self-belief. That goes back to preparation. Are you mentally, emotionally, and physically preparing to play your best golf? Are you ready to confront your shame, and consciously work on the issues that torment you? Without the drive to understand the source of your shame and to stare at your own trauma in a way that helps to acknowledge, then create a different relationship to this trauma, you are likely to stay in this circle of stored trauma and shame. In his book *The Body Keeps the Score*, renowned Dutch-American author, researcher, and psychiatrist Bessel van der Kolk offers many tips to help relieve trauma. The key principle is to recognize trauma as a global insult to our bodies. It requires work on your mental and emotional state of mind, your physical health, and your social environment. That's a lot, but it's worth it. Physical therapies like yoga or breathing exercises and movement can help dislodge the physical impact of trauma. I'm all for therapy, but quite often, therapy is not enough.

Shame that comes from trauma can often result in isolation. So the process involves not only owning the trauma—understanding you lived through it—but not allowing it to define you. It involves developing compassion for yourself so that you can integrate yourself back into your community. The final goal becomes to reclaim yourself, your identity, and define yourself by how you *handled* your trauma, not by the trauma itself.

Part of the process of flushing shame from the brain can start with forgiveness. Forgive yourself for the drive you yanked into the woods. Forgive yourself for the doubts planted in you by old role models, parents, teachers, coaches, or whoever. Just because someone didn't believe in you doesn't mean you can't believe in yourself. This applies to my player who hits an errant shot and has to attempt the next one from a terrible lie. It equally applies to my client who is leading a sales meeting for her staff and wants to express her wisdom and provide leadership for her team even though doubt had been sown in her as a child, when she was told she wasn't bright enough to lead. The golfer needs to flush the shame from the bad shot and give full commitment to the next one. The exec needs to identify that the labels placed on her by others don't define her capabilities in that meeting. Dealing with shame and our past trauma is essential if we are to find a new path that is fulfilling for both professions.

What's important to remember is that shame is, at base, an extremely human quality. We shouldn't run from it. We should examine it and trace it to its roots so we can learn how to expunge it—and rebuild our self-belief. It's in there somewhere.

# Chapter 8

# Anger

*"Of all the hazards, fear and anger are the worst."*
—Sam Snead

A friend of mine played in a tournament that was absolutely supposed to be for fun. This is an amateur player, a weekend high-handicapper for whom golf is very much an avocation, something he looks forward to and a means to get his mind off of other things—as it is for so many of us. I bet you have encountered the person that defined his foursome that day. Maybe you have even *been* the person who defined his foursome that day.

In this "just-for-fun" event, this playing partner grew extraordinarily hard on himself almost from the first hole. By midway through the front nine, he was cursing—loudly. By the turn, he had thrown a club. On the back nine, he would throw more. A poor shot was followed by yelling, then by a seething walk up the fairway. He was so full of anger, so uncontrollably letting it out for all to hear, that he made the round miserable not just for himself, but for his playing partners. The tournament was anything but fun. It became an exercise in soothing this guy's ego and trying to get him to simmer down.

Anger often seems to be right beneath the surface in golf. That's sad given the vast majority of us think of a round as a time to relax and enjoy ourselves. It's something we anticipate with joy. Why would we let it upset us so badly? Indeed, managing anger is a major part of my job in working with PGA Tour players and executives alike. A tour player's anger is on display for everyone to see. We know who has thrown clubs on the course. We know who flings balls into the water. Managing one's feelings can be a foundation of life if we choose. Our abilities to use intense emotions lead to focus in certain situations. Sometimes, in the process of climbing a mountain, we can plateau, slip backward, or accelerate upward. It is a journey. It's never a straight line.

When I talk about anger with a client, I really want to get to its root cause. But first, we do a simple exercise. We have talked about shame and embarrassment and whether we would feel those emotions if we were playing golf on a deserted island and we shanked a shot. Apply that same drill to anger. We have all either gotten furious with ourselves or seen a playing partner storm around because a shot or hole went awry. But would our actions and reactions be the same if we were playing all by ourselves, with no one around to see what happened?

So many of my clients say, "No way." I find that fascinating. I have also discussed this idea with my clients who are extremely into video games. As silly as it might sound, these people have goals they want to reach and levels they want to achieve in those games. They're often competing against other people online, so in some ways it's not that different from playing in a golf tournament. But down to a person, they tell me they just don't get angry over their failure to achieve the next step in a shoot-'em-up computer game. "It's just a game," one of them told me. "It's just entertainment." Wouldn't it be great to channel that kind of energy into the pursuits that matter?

We don't play golf on deserted islands, though, and we have far more important quests than video games that define our lives at home and at work. Yes, some of us may sneak out for a solo round from time to time. (What a treat!) And yes, even in those situations, maybe we become frustrated because we're not playing well. Our standard is our standard, and part of being a fully actualized person is being able to handle situations the same way whether someone is watching or not.

But the idea that we grow angry with ourselves when other people are around is worth exploring. As with so many emotions, it's unwise to suppress anger. I had a mentor tell me that depression is anger turned inward. I think about that a lot. As we have discussed previously, it's no problem to get angry in the moment after a bad shot as long as we're equipped with a pathway to reach a more stable emotional state fairly quickly. It's the old 30-second rule (or 60 seconds, or 5 minutes, or whatever). Feel the anger for five seconds if you duffed your drive, but then reset. The first step to resetting is, of course, being aware that you're angry. No outburst can be subdued without awareness. Acknowledge that you're angry. "I flubbed that chip. Now I can't save par. That pisses me off." You can be mad—briefly, with a strict time limit, as we've discussed. You just can't get down. There's a difference, and it's important.

That sounds so obvious, and it's so tied in to much of what we have explored in earlier parts of this book. But it also requires self-awareness and intentional thinking that can be hard to access when we're upset with ourselves. That means we have to train our brains to not just *be* angry when something goes wrong. We have to train ourselves to be able to step outside our bodies, to see ourselves growing angry. And we have to understand that anger can absolutely affect our performance. It affects us physically. Our muscles can tense up. We can overswing, trying to murder the ball. It affects us mentally, too. Have you ever walked to a tee box saying you absolutely have to make par because of the double bogey you just hacked out on the previous hole? You're angry, and rather than focusing on the next shot and only the next shot, your anger is steering your thoughts to places they shouldn't go—trying to make up for what happened by putting pressure on what's next.

It's important not only to deal with anger in the moment by equipping ourselves with tools that help us first acknowledge it and then move past it. It's also imperative that—when the round is over and the emotion has been flushed out of our brains—we step back and think, "Where is that coming from? Is there a way to redirect it?" While you can use a tool to control your anger in the moment, the middle of a round of golf or an important meeting is not really a time to reflect. The reflection, though, should come later, and when it does, it should be honest and deep.

Do you get angry during a round because your expectations are too high? Are you a bogey golfer who expects to string pars together and grows rattled when you don't? Are you carrying issues from other aspects of your life onto the golf course and allowing them to affect both your play and your mood? Are you disappointed in yourself, or worried that others are disappointed in you? There are almost endless possibilities. Exploring the root causes of your anger can not only help you control it in the moment but aid you in reducing or even eliminating outbursts. It is important to mention here that my favorite stat on the PGA Tour is the Bounce Back stat. This is when you make a birdie after a bogey. What a beautiful opportunity to "go get it back" by resetting and refocusing. This is a great example of using everything that happens, everything for our growth and success, on and off the course.

This is important for our own successful performance and, of course, our own well-being. But it's also important for everyone around us—on the golf course, at home, at work. Anger is an emotion that can have its roots in shame or embarrassment. It's also different from shame or embarrassment. Those emotions are directed inward. Anger that bursts to the surface can bring down the entire room. That's true in a golf foursome. It's true in a team locker room. It's true in a boardroom. Anger isn't always just a personal experience. It can often be a shared experience. That's so important for us to realize, because managing our anger doesn't just help ourselves. It helps everyone who might be in our presence at that moment.

• • •

In December 2009, I was working with the Washington Wizards, the NBA team in the city where I live. Being a mental coach who is hired by a professional sports team can be difficult. The players can be reluctant to speak candidly about their issues and emotions because they can view you as a mole for management. Trust is harder to build because there can be suspicions about who you're sharing their stories with. Why would the executives of a franchise care about players' emotional and mental well-being when the athletes are just cogs in the machine? It's surprising how often players can resent and resist coaches whose job it is to maximize their performance and lead the team to wins.

My job with the Wizards was to help get them to communicate better. That's so much different from working with an individual golfer. Rather than dealing with just one person's thoughts and beliefs and the inner workings of their brains, helping a team communicate depends on the skill sets and intellects of people from all sorts of backgrounds. It can be hard to find a common language even as the individual players understand how important relationships are in building a team.

We worked at it, though. We set goals as individuals and each player identified goals for the team. We talked about how to support each other as teammates while developing ourselves. It was almost like working as a marriage counselor, trying to figure out ways that players with different personalities and sensibilities could talk to each other. I thought we were actually starting to make progress.

Within a team, though, there can also be tension. Gilbert Arenas, the Wizards' star guard back then, had something of a rivalry with Javaris Crittenton, one of his teammates. I noticed it as I worked with the group. I didn't understand its depths. On a flight back from a road trip that December, the two got into an argument over a card game. At issue: $1,100. Arenas's contract at the time was due to pay him $111 million over six years. The anger that bubbled, then, wasn't really about the money, right? When I arrived for practice two days later, I had no idea about the dispute that arose on the plane nor how heated it had become. And I had no idea what I was about to get into.

It was clear, as players gathered for practice in the locker room that day, that Arenas was angry. Then he revealed exactly how serious he was about his emotions: He turned around at his locker and revealed four guns. My memory of what transpired is hazy. I was definitely scared—and remember that so many of the players who stopped in their tracks seemed scared, too.

"Hey, MF, come pick one," Arenas said to Crittenton, according to the memoir of Caron Butler, a Wizards teammate and team leader at the time. "I'm going to shoot your ass with one of these."

"Oh no, you don't need to shoot me with one of those," Crittenton responded. In Butler's telling, Crittenton turned around "slowly like a gunslinger in the Old West," and then said, "I've got one right here."

Crittenton pointed a pistol at Arenas. It was loaded.

I thought somebody was going to get hurt. I thought somebody was going to get shot. I thought somebody might die.

We all scattered. Butler, who grew up in a rough neighborhood in Racine, Wisconsin, was left to defuse the matter. He spoke calmly to Crittenton, who slowly lowered his gun. Arenas left the scene. The chaos went no further.

•   •   •

That's a pretty dramatic and unique way to show how the anger of just one or two people can affect an entire team. To my knowledge, players haven't confronted each other with guns in an NBA locker room before or since. This was isolated—serious and scary, for sure, but not something we'd see on the golf course, in another locker room, or at the office, hopefully.

The point, though, holds: Our anger isn't just about ourselves. Anger, more than just about any other emotion, can have a severe impact on those around us.

In a team dynamic, it's particularly important that we take responsibility for our own anger. You're not allowed to drag down the vibe of a group with collective goals just because you're having a bad day. We have to understand that anger can penetrate the rest of the room and impact the performance of others. That's true if you're leading a meeting, because an angry and tense tenor infiltrates the entire group. My husband's uncle was known to say, "The tone of your voice is ruining the tenor of my day." It's also true as a participant in a meeting who is being led by others. Anger is powerful enough that it can be both hard to hide and can seep from one member of a team into the rest of the people present, regardless of the angry person's role in the group.

Basketball is, of course, a sport that moves more quickly than golf. One play is connected to the next with no time in between. But it's amazing how quickly one player's anger—over a bad call by a referee, over a missed shot, over a teammate's unwillingness to pass them the ball, over a lack of playing time—can immediately become apparent to his teammates and just as quickly become detrimental to the team. You see it in body language on the court or in the huddle. There's nothing worse than a mopey, ticked-off teammate. That behavior is insidious. It can spread like a brushfire. It kind of makes you want to say to the angry person, "Hey, buddy. Look how *your* attitude is affecting *all* of us!"

That's actually an important piece in our relationship with anger. It isn't always our own anger that affects performance. Think about my friend who was playing with the angry guy in that amateur tournament. He felt helpless, and his playing partner's anger impacted his own game. This happens in all sorts of areas of golf. Is a member of the group growing angry because someone else is playing so slowly? Does another player feel rushed? Is there resentment building because someone took an overly generous drop or another player claimed to find a ball that was obviously sent deep into the woods? In those situations, does anger have to take over the entire day? Or might we have tools we could deploy to help a person who's exploding—and therefore help the rest of the group or the team?

Of course we can assemble those tools. But to use them, we have to find our voice. This can be difficult in a team environment. It demands some level of self-confidence and a willingness to risk being perceived as overstepping your bounds. But think about the alternative: If a club-throwing madman is cursing his way through your round, and therefore diminishing the performance of an entire foursome, *not* saying something increases the possibility that his anger at himself morphs into your anger at him. Who wins then?

If you have a regular playing partner who behaves badly, it might be better to arm yourself with some devices for defusing the situation early in the day. Maybe it's a lighthearted joke that's ready for the first club toss. Maybe it's a hand on the shoulder and a quiet word that it's going to be a long day for everyone if their behavior continues to trend downward. Maybe it's figuring out a conversation that would allow them to deflect the anger and refocus. And maybe it's a gentle reminder of something we should all bring to every round of golf and so many other situations, too: The environment we create on the tee box or in the conference room is our own responsibility. And if we know that we have buttons that can be pressed—we're annoyed by slow play or chatty playing partners or whatever—it's up to us to be aware of those buttons and deal with them when they're pressed by others.

There are examples in business, too, in which finding a way to talk openly with a coworker or a boss can help defuse anger that is building. I work with an executive who was struggling with a new boss. She felt that despite her experience with her company and her rise to a prominent and important role, he talked down to her too often. (There may be some male-female dynamics at work here, but that's another subject.) She was growing angry at him, and not just because he was belittling her in front of others. His dismissiveness was preventing her from maximizing her output and making the contributions she expected of herself. She felt like she hadn't equipped herself with a way to challenge someone above her in a healthy and honest way. It's up to us as individuals to reframe that anger and deal with it elsewhere. She hadn't found her voice—one that's so essential not only in ridding yourself of building anger but in dissipating anger that could filter throughout a team.

For professional golfers, anger can be more deeply rooted because the results of each shot, each round, and each tournament are directly tied to how successful they are in their careers. For them, a bogey on the final hole on a Friday could mean missing the cut by a single shot, and missing the cut means the difference between making hundreds of thousands of dollars and—nothing. Zilch. The stakes are high, so the anger over their performance can seem justifiable.

That said, I've had so many conversations with my clients over the years about their outward expressions of anger on the course and how detrimental it can be to their results—both in a specific round and in the long view. Club-smashing and club-tossing now tend to go viral. People love watching the best in the world endure such emotional reactions to mistakes we all make, and we live in a world in which news is consumed through small slices of video. In a talk about allowing anger out on the course, one of my clients said, "It shows people how much I want it."

I thought that was interesting. Can anger build within us because we're worried about disappointing other people? For professional golfers, that could be the ticket-buyers who come to see them perform or the sponsors who pay them good money to wear their logos and, in turn, represent them in the most positive way possible. Smashing a club onto a tee box is, ahem, not representing a company in the most positive way possible. As I've told so many of my clients: That's no way to be a champion.

But because anger is real and powerful, we have to find a way to bring ourselves back to neutral—and quickly. Yes, I know golf swing coaches who don't mind if their players "run hot." We have seen players channel the frustration from a sloppy bogey or a wayward swing into a string of birdies. Heck, maybe we have done something similar ourselves. Again, I'm not suggesting we suppress our anger. Maybe allowing anger to fuel us for a hole or a round can be productive. But as I've said before: I really don't believe that running hot is a good long-term strategy or a healthy way to live our lives.

Think about those emotions and reactions off the golf course. I talked with one of my clients about road rage—a real version of what we have discussed, a reaction to something that upsets us. This guy had someone cut him off on the highway, and he's a guy who tends to run hot. His response: Speed up and chase the guy down the highway. To what end? Who is that serving?

Which brings up an even more important aspect of dealing with anger, the mantra for how we might confront it that applies to so many areas we have already explored: It's not the issue. It's the way we relate to the issue.

Think about that with slow play. Think about that with the driver who cuts you off. The negative impact on our life doesn't happen because a playing partner stood over the ball for three minutes or because some random car darted in front of us. The negative impact arrives only from how we respond to what happened. Do we fly into a rage ourselves? Or do we have a way to remain neutral, to observe what happened, and to let it slide quietly into our past?

Here's a quick story about another friend. In Washington, D.C., as in so many cities, the proliferation of meal delivery by restaurants during the pandemic persisted long thereafter and gave rise to an army of scooter and moped drivers who zoom their way all over the city. They would drive this friend crazy—running through red lights, zipping between lines of cars, not even considering the most basic traffic rules. He would be driving his teenage daughter around, ranting and raving about the insane scooters and how dangerous they were. One day, the daughter turned to him and said, "Daddy, I know you find them infuriating. I've heard it a million times. You have to find a way not to go into a diatribe about them every single time. Could you come up with a single word to use instead?"

With that, they decided on "Egg." Why? Who knows? Doesn't matter. What's important: Every time a delivery moped cut my friend off, instead of spiraling into a rage about it, he simply said out loud, "Egg." It worked. What a great example of taking the issue and determining how we relate to it. Instantly, my friend's drives around the city flipped from angry and stressful to something he could laugh about with his kid. He still chuckles every time a scooter snakes between traffic and he responds by muttering, "Egg."

That's a small example. Anger is a big issue. How we relate to it is important in both our performance and our mental health. As with most issues in this book and in my work, I believe it's helpful to go back and examine your life to find the root causes of your anger. One way to do that is to consider how we developed as children and young adults, and what parts of us might have had difficulty evolving as we aged.

Erik Erikson was a famous psychologist who developed eight stages that help us explain and chart psychosocial development. They started with "Trust vs. Mistrust," which is what we learn from the time we're born until we're about eighteen months old. They move through such stages as "Autonomy vs. Shame and Doubt," "Initiative vs. Guilt," "Industry vs. Inferiority," and "Identity vs. Role Confusion" as we move into adulthood. Working deeply on ourselves can help identify whether we got stuck in one of those early stages. We didn't learn how to be autonomous, or we never developed the instinct to take initiative. We felt inferior to our peers, and that prevented us from becoming productive workers or team members. We never truly learned who we were.

I understand that people could be skeptical about dividing our lives up into manageable chunks. But I believe the root of anger can be traced back to someone becoming stuck in any one of those stages of social and emotional development. Therefore, it's important that we identify the buttons we all carry around that can be pressed by others and spark negative emotions and reactions within ourselves. Take me: My biggest button is being lied to. It could be about a golf score. It could be at home or at work. It could be a waitress or a clerk. I know that because I was raised in an environment in which my mother lied to me not a little, but all the time, lying is something that is going to trigger anger in me. My husband? If he was told a lie, he'd likely either not notice or would flip the situation around: "Why would I care? That's about them."

Let's review a few ways to deal with anger when it surfaces on the golf course—or in our everyday lives:

- **Be aware:** When you begin to feel angry, acknowledge it. Note it. Only then can you bring yourself back to neutral and focus on the next shot, the next hole, or the next appointment in your workday. This can and should happen in the moment.
- **Evaluate and explore:** After an event that made you angry, take time to calm down and revisit what happened. Where is the anger coming from? Was it about what happened in the round of golf, or were you bringing baggage to that round? This exercise is best undertaken with some distance from the event.
- **Develop your voice:** Find ways to stand up for yourself when the actions of others cause anger to grow within you. Can you politely encourage the club-tosser in your group to understand how his actions impact others? Can

you confidently but appropriately stand up in a meeting and constructively push back on a superior's idea when you believe you have a better one rather than quietly seething?

- **It's not the issue. It's how we relate to the issue:** Think about when you get angry and how you respond. Was there a way to acknowledge the behavior of someone else but not internalize it? Can you come up with a tool that allows you to identify what happened but not spiral out of control?

- **Know your buttons:** Understanding what makes us angry can help us head off anger before it begins to rage out of control. Think about what triggers you and how you might react to make things better both as events happen and for your long-term mental health.

Let's go back one last time to my friend and the cursing, club-throwing playing partner. My friend left that round having been negatively affected by this jerk's behavior. But he had also allowed himself to be a victim. Anger in one player begat anger in another. That's not a solution for anyone. There were no winners.

What's important for any of us is to gain awareness that our actions and emotions have an impact on others. We know, in any sort of competition, adversaries might try to play mind games against each other. In golf or at work, it's up to each of us to make sure that any outside influences on our decision-making or performance aren't the responsibilities of the other people involved. They're on us. We can decide to be angry, or we can deflect that emotion and use it to get us into a more productive headspace. What matters isn't the event that just happened that ticked us off. What matters is how we deal with it and move on. It's a matter of personal responsibility that has a deep impact on everyone around you.

You have to arrive at that first tee box, look your playing partners in the eye, and figure out—in a moment of frustration—how *not* to throw that club. Because it's not just about you.

Chapter 9

# Your Best Competitive State

*"I am the greatest, I said that even before I knew I was."*
—Muhammad Ali

I was working with a client who was preparing to run the New York City Marathon. What a different pursuit from golf, right? It's not relaxing. It's grueling. The physical challenge is daunting. But the mental challenge might be greater. You're going to have moments when you're thinking about a twinge in your knee or a stitch in your side. You're going to have moments when you think, "I'm only at mile ten?" You're going to have moments when you're dreading the uphill climb ahead. Any marathoner must be prepared for all those strides over 26.2 miles. It's cardiovascular endurance, for sure. But any marathoner must be prepared for the moments when they question themselves, too. Maybe that's more intimidating. It's almost certainly more important.

In that sense, working with a mental coach is the same in running as it is in golf—as it is at work in a boardroom. Challenges can't be overcome if we wait to deal with them when they arise. We have to be ready for those challenging moments in advance so when they inevitably surface, we know how to handle them. We're prepared. That's what so much of this work is about: Training our brains so that when times get tough, we don't spiral downward and lose control. We're equipped to deal with the circumstances. That's in a round of golf. That's running a marathon. That's in the middle of a project at work. Adversity can bring grit.

Think about it this way: Working with a mental coach—or reading this book—comes with a clear objective. We're trying to prepare your brain to be ready when the coach isn't there and the book is back on a nightstand. I can't be with my players in the middle of a round in a tournament. I can't stand by an executive client while she's giving a speech. You can't pull this book from your golf bag and look at a list of tools that might help you put behind a bad hole or a terrible swing. All of the helpful behaviors we lean on in those moments must become ingrained. They must become hardwired. That's only possible if we do the work beforehand.

In doing that work, the basic question is this: For you individually, what brings out your best competitive state? And what can you do in advance to make sure that when the time comes, you can call on the training to get you into that mindset?

This is a process, one of self-discovery. I believe it's rooted in digging deep into our past, as we've discussed. The variety of ways to go about that is part of what I find so fascinating and fun about working with athletes and executives from different sports and lines of work, each with their own personalities and preferences, their own objectives and hopes. It's not important that any client or reader follows my instructions or suggestions to the letter. It's important that every individual figures out what works for them. The goals are the same: Be present and focused. Know how to overcome a setback and get back to neutral or better quickly. These skills allow us to execute the task at hand, be it a golf shot or the next mile in a marathon or the closing anecdote in a speech. The paths to get there vary widely, which is great, because it all becomes part of the process of truly knowing ourselves.

In that sense, we can look for tools that might work for us as individuals everywhere around us. They can pop up at any time. I was watching the US Open—not golf, but tennis—on television, without a client on site or a stake in the outcome of any match. In the men's semifinals, American Taylor Fritz was playing Serbian legend Novak Djokovic, one of the best players in the history of the sport. The match was competitive, and I found myself enthralled with Fritz's method for putting behind a point and moving on to the next one. If he committed an unforced error or missed a shot, Fritz would kind of yank his racquet immediately and yell to himself, "Come on!" I loved it. It wasn't with a tone of, "Come on, you idiot!" It was much more, "Come on, you got this!" It was clear that phrase was a tool he had equipped himself with in order to get back to a neutral state—or better—and move on to the next point.

In a sense, that kind of mechanism might be labeled "positive self-talk." It fits with another piece of advice I hear, and sometimes even give: "Be your own cheerleader." Both of those phrases acknowledge that in sports such as golf and tennis—or in business if we're giving a presentation or leading a meeting—there's no coach, guru, or crutch to lean on (except ourselves) in the heat of competition. We have to be able to provide our own methods of getting our brains back into the right headspace. That ability doesn't come from anybody else, and it isn't realized in the moment. It comes from our preparation that we use to create a good foundation from which we can compete. You must do the mental work before the moment when you need to pull (draw) on it. Then you must be able to rely on yourself for motivation and focus, cheering yourself forward.

I should admit something, though: As much as I sometimes advise clients that their thinking should be positive, that they should spend time acknowledging that they're grateful to be in the moment competing, I don't love the terms "positive" or "cheerleader" for everyone. They're a little squishy. It almost sounds as if forcing a smile on your face will make everything better. It's lovey-dovey, kind of a false happiness. And that's the *opposite* of what we're going for when we're talking about being prepared for challenging moments and bringing out our best competitive state. You can't *pretend* to be positive and in a neutral or better state. Your brain has to be trained to get there, and you can't fake the preparation. Plus, we all know athletes who are at their competitive best when they're a little ticked off or downright angry. I'm not going to advise clients like that to turn into happy-go-lucky cheerleaders for themselves when they're actually better with a little edge. Whatever works.

If you have done the preparation—not just over a few days, but over months and years—the tools that work for you will be there to draw on. I have clients tell me all the time, "I didn't practice enough this week. I'm not prepared." That could be true leading up to a specific tournament. Life has a tendency to get in the way of golf. Kids need attention. The house is under repair. You had a dentist appointment. Even when playing golf is your profession, working on your game can feel like you're shirking other duties. It happens to all of us at every level of the game.

But in reality, that line of thinking by these pros—"I'm not prepared"—is just their brains playing tricks on them. It can happen to you, too, if not on the golf course—where you probably haven't put in as much time as a touring pro—then at work. You have spent your whole professional life building a foundation that has prepared you for the most important moments in your job, whatever that job might be. That's true of the golfers. When they say they haven't prepared enough, I'll remind them they're being very narrow- and small-minded. They have to think more broadly, because they have all the information they need. "You are going to step to the first tee, and you can tell me exactly where you want to hit it and how you're going to execute the shot." Don't buy into the idea that a blip in preparation wipes out years of work. It doesn't.

Let's think about ways we can build that foundation and make sure that we can reach our best competitive mindset when we need to. We have talked about all sorts of tools that can help us return to the moment, to shake our anger, to move on from a discouraging development. Taylor Fritz yelling, "Come on!" at himself. A golfer patting his head cover or listening to the Velcro on his golf glove. Those are all useful. They're also small. What about something bigger, deeper, more meaningful?

•   •   •

One more foundational tool we haven't yet discussed can be, for so many people, among the most important: Meditation.

In the staid world of professional golf, meditation still carries with it a certain reputation. Even as it has become mainstream for so many people, it can be considered kind of woo-woo out on tour. A lot of people link it with Buddhism because it is such an integral part of how Buddhists anchor (or free) themselves. In Buddhism, meditation is used to transform the mind. The techniques encourage and develop concentration, clarity, emotional positivity, and calmness. Buddhists believe that with regular work, your mind can develop new habits, and you can evolve into someone who views the world more positively and with more altitude. The practice can help the mind focus better and become profoundly peaceful. Buddhists believe meditation helps people better understand life.

But you don't have to be Buddhist to meditate, and meditating doesn't make you a Buddhist. I believe in it. I recommend it and teach it to clients of all religions and backgrounds, but it doesn't at all have to be attached to religion. There shouldn't be a stigma around it. For so many people, it helps. For so many people, it works.

One way I start with meditation is to keep it simple. "Box breathing," which we discussed early on, is almost a gateway to meditation. There are also tons of apps you can download to your phone that provide "guided" meditations, someone to hold your hand and walk you through the process. Calm, Headspace, and Insight Timer are just a few of the apps that my clients use to get started. They often continue with them even when they become more experienced meditators. Guided meditations can help someone new to the practice to just sit back or lie down and follow instructions. There's no religious attachment. There's no mantra to repeat. You're just learning how to bring your brain back to the present. The list of things swirling in your mind—the groceries you have to buy or the dog you have to walk or the parent-teacher conference you have to schedule—melts away. It could be simply by listening to your breath. Working through guided meditations can help your brain tap into a calm, present state that you then may be able to access in competition or under pressure at work.

Meditation brings the body and the brain to a relaxed state in the moment you're doing it. But it also serves as preparation to reach something close to that state when your eyes are open and you're processing a challenging situation. Its benefits are both in the short- and long-term.

Meditation must be a commitment, but it doesn't have to take up tons of time. My clients usually start with 10- or 15-minute sessions that are easy to follow and execute. The guide might ask you to draw in a deep breath, hold it, and then let it out slowly—similar to the "box breathing" method we have already discussed. It then might add on small body movements—wiggle your toes, open your palms, execute a few simple motions that get you consciously connected to your body's current state. I recommend that you begin by thinking about someone or something you love. That quietly and subtly urges you to consciously steer your thoughts—or even better, let them go. Like clouds moving across the sky, let your thoughts come in one ear and out the other. This is training you for when you're in that board meeting or when you're facing a difficult approach shot. You can feel how relaxed you become when you're taking those deep breaths and doing something like wiggling your toes, which could seem silly. If you have done it during meditation, there's a better chance you can rediscover those feelings when you need to slip into your best competitive state. It's almost like a rehearsal. If you might think, "I can't miss this putt," let that thought go. If you're going to hold on to any thought at all, let it be a positive one. "This putt is dropping."

Meditation is a way of releasing tension and bad thoughts. Start here: I know for me, as a 14-handicapper, when I'm nervous on the golf course I have major muscle tension. That's not exclusive to me. It's a pretty common reaction to nerves and stress. We know muscle tension is bad for most of our golf swings. In those moments, I can feel my shoulders rise up around my ears. When that happens, I can draw on my meditations, breathing deeply, exhaling, and doing a little body movement that releases that tension. I've trained my brain to help my body when it seems like it's inhibiting me.

If you've meditated, you're better prepared to recognize that tension and get your muscles to relax.

This is mindfulness, the relationship between internal and environmental consciousness. Meditation can help us to be aware of ourselves and our environment more acutely. I can't release my muscle tension if I'm not aware my muscles are tense. So much of the work we do comes back to that point: Are we aware of what we're doing, how we're acting, how we're feeling? If we struggle with becoming self-aware, how can we equip ourselves with tools to get there? Meditation can be central in that pursuit.

We might think of the setting for meditation being a dimly lit or dark room. We might lie on a rug or sit in a lounge chair. There are also classic meditation poses rooted in Buddhism—the quarter lotus or half lotus, where we sit with our legs crossed. A traditional Buddha statue will almost always have his legs folded underneath him. We might also think about hand positions, which in Buddhism are called "mudras" and are used in various forms of yoga. Mudras have many symbolic meanings, but in yoga or meditation, they're meant to help stimulate parts of the body.

It's true that we want to be comfortable when we meditate. But it's also true that you don't have to get into a position which you might associate with classic meditation in order to meditate. When you practice meditation over time, you can do it just about anywhere. In my view, you *should* learn to do it just about anywhere. Meditation shouldn't be about a specific setting. It should be about a specific mindset. If we can only use it to calm and center ourselves in one place, how can we access those feelings when we're under pressure in competition?

When I first started to get into meditation, I was on a road trip with some other women. We were in the car, and the woman in the back seat said, "Guys, I'm going to take a little break and meditate for a bit."

Seriously? I was like, "Can the rest of us keep chatting and just continue our conversation? Or do you need us to be quiet?" My friend actually encouraged us to keep talking so she could practice using distraction to help her get quiet inside. We listened to the news.

It's a great reminder that your physical environment and positioning don't matter as much as your mindset does. Yes, you can get in your most comfortable chair and turn off your phone and have no stimulation. That works as surroundings in which to meditate, and it's a great place to start. But you can also pull off what could be seen as mini meditations three minutes before your board meeting or as you walk down the fairway. For a professional golfer or other athlete, there might even be benefits to meditating in an environment that's hectic or chaotic. Take Grand Central Station. Sit down on a bench. Note the swarms of people scurrying in every direction, the announcements over the public address system, the lights on shops and restaurants, the changing of the giant schedule boards. It's almost overwhelming. Now, meditate. Breathe deeply. Take note of your body position. Feel your toes wiggle or your fingers drum. If you're able to return your body to a neutral or better position in such a cacophony, then doing so with galleries watching and cheering will come more naturally. A pro golfer might think of playing at the Ryder Cup as his sport's busiest, loudest train station. Meditating could prepare him to perform in that environment.

We think of meditation as brain training, and it is. But it's important to note that there is an array of physical benefits to the practice, too. Like the intentional breathing methods we have already discussed, meditation can help lower blood pressure. Scientific studies show it reduces stress and anxiety. The National Academy of Sciences found that meditation can help reduce addictive behaviors, such as smoking cigarettes. A study published in the *American Journal of Psychiatry* shows that meditation can help people deal with chronic pain.

Meditation is more widely accepted and practiced now than it ever has been, particularly among high-performing athletes. But the scientific backing of some of its religious roots dates back at least half a century. The 1975 book *The Relaxation Response* was written by a Harvard physician named Herbert Benson and his writing partner, Miriam Z. Klipper. Benson agreed to study practitioners of Transcendental Meditation (or TM), which is an ancient meditation practice that involves saying a mantra or repeating a sound. Benson's study found that meditation could reduce a person's metabolic rate within minutes of beginning a session. Further studies showed that people with high blood pressure could lower their blood pressure significantly by meditating over a period of time.

You can see how much I believe in meditation as a process that helps us arrive in our best competitive state more regularly and easily. It may have roots in Eastern religion, but it is accessible to everyone with any belief system. It takes a commitment to doing it regularly, or else the state we're seeking won't be available when we need it most. Working on your mental health should be like going to the gym or monitoring your diet. It takes effort. For those who want to meditate, it can be 5 to 10 minutes or 30 to 60 minutes you spend on your mental health every day. But of the tools with which I try to equip my clients, it can be among the most important. It's deep. It's foundational. It's centering. It's calming. It can be such a benefit to our minds and our bodies. Why not at least try it?

◆　◆　◆

I do some pro bono work with the men's and women's golf teams at Howard University, the historically Black college in Washington, D.C., where NBA superstar Steph Curry agreed to partly fund the golf programs. In one of our group sessions, a player lamented how much he loathed a competitor in his group at a tournament. We have discussed all kinds of distracting playing partners and ways to deal with them. This kid was aware he was supposed to be playing the course, not the annoying guy in his group.

I could hear how flipped out this player was. The frustration in his voice was palpable. So I said, "Listen, I might be totally off base here. But what if you just channeled your energy into beating the guy? No, don't hit him over the head with a golf club. But destroying him competitively."

The kid lit up. "Oh my God," he said. "That's when I play my best!"

Look, we know I don't believe in playing from a position of anger, and I wouldn't suggest that approach or thought for everybody. It's a weird mindset to bring up after spending so much time on the relaxing benefits of meditation. But this chapter isn't about getting every single type of personality to meditate. I have accomplished professionals who just can't get themselves to take meditation seriously. As much as I believe in the practice, I believe even more strongly in the idea that every individual has to find her or his own path to their best competitive state. Examine your life. Examine your brain. Be aware of who you are. Find what works for you. This kid's best competitive state: Screw you, opponent. I bet you can think of some pro golfers or athletes who embody that, too.

Almost the opposite can be true for some other people. For years on the PGA Tour there have been deeply Christian players. Some of them would describe themselves as "Born Again." Over the course of the grind of the season—when travel and competition and life can wear on anyone—they tend to meet on Wednesday nights before tournaments. Their religion serves as a sanctuary for them. It helps ground them.

The most modern iteration of this group shows up on a podcast called *The Bible Caddie*, which is cohosted by long-time PGA Tour players Webb Simpson and Ben Crane along with a minister named William Kane. They often have other PGA Tour players on as guests. I find it to be fascinating listening. I'm Jewish, but I listen to their posts and podcasts all the time. The talk often falls back on how these players don't go dark or spiral negatively out of control or even feel much pain because they believe Jesus Christ has saved them. That belief serves as a guiding force, a backbone to their lives. They discuss it with those who will listen. It gives them a real safety net against all the tendencies of our minds to go to bad places if we haven't trained them to do otherwise.

You can believe Jesus will forgive us for all our sins or not. You can be anchored in the idea that we have eternal life or think that's a hoax. You can be a regular reader and student of the Bible or never have cracked it open even once. The point is: Those beliefs work for the guys on *The Bible Caddie* and their listeners. They know themselves. They're aware of who they are and how to access their best versions. Again, it comes back to whatever works.

To that point: When I'm talking to a prospective new client, I usually ask them a binary question: Do I have to get you going or do I have to calm you down?

Think about that for yourself. Do you need motivation to get better at golf or at work? Or are you so jacked up that you need your heart rate to come down? I have seen it both ways on the PGA Tour. I have some clients—usually the most accomplished players—who find the first rounds of tournaments to be almost impossibly boring. There's nothing really at stake. The event can't be won on Thursday. Sunday seems so far away. Who cares?

Then there's another set that puts their tees in the ground on Thursday morning, and their minds can't wait to get to Sunday. They have 72 holes to play, and they're already thinking about the final nine. They're almost inherently incapable of making themselves present because their minds are spinning off to what might happen in the days ahead.

Neither approach is particularly helpful. But either can be dealt with. The point here is that we're not trying to put anybody in a box. We want everybody to discover their own box, and then dig into it. If you're playing a round of golf, how do you—not anybody else, but *you*—become the most committed and focused over every shot? If you're running a marathon, how do you get your mind to enjoy the next stride, the next mile, the next hill rather than dreading the obstacles ahead? If you're making a presentation, how do you access your most dynamic, engaging self? In order to achieve your best competitive state, you have to know yourself.

To review, here are some steps that can help you figure out how to access the mental space from which you compete best:

- **Learn yourself:** Study and acknowledge how you feel when you're at your competitive best. Are you better when you're a little nervous? Do you need to be completely calm? What happens when your muscles get tense? Understanding your brain and your body when you're *not* in the pressure of competition will help you access your best frame of mind when you need it.
- **Learn to meditate:** Try guided meditations to get started. Figure out what environment works for you. Work on deep breathing and conscious relaxing of your body. Understand how the practice calms both the body and the mind.

- **Learn to bring meditation to the golf course or boardroom:** Take the meditation methods you used in an environment devoid of stimulation and deploy them in areas where you could be easily distracted. This could be in a busy airport terminal or on the golf course. Understand how the skills you learned in the quiet of your own home can be translated to environments where you might need to draw on them under pressure.

- **Learn to make mental health part of your routine:** This can't be lip service. Acknowledge that tending to your mental health is every bit as important as working out your body. Create habits that help your mind build a foundation. Understand the tools that work best for you and practice using them before you need them under fire.

Chapter 10

# Success and Setbacks

*"It's not whether you get knocked down. It's whether you get up."*
—Vince Lombardi

On the Thursday afternoon of the 2025 Players Championship, a signature event played on the famous TPC Sawgrass course in Ponte Vedra Beach, Florida, I sat on the grass in the out-of-the-way back practice range and chatted with Justin Thomas as he hit ball after ball after ball—after ball after ball after ball.

Justin is one of the world's best players, and he holds himself to incredibly high standards in terms of performance. That day, in the first round of the Players, he shot 78. Only six players in the field were worse. He arrived at his eighth hole of the day at 2 under par. This was the famous par-3 17th with the island green. He hit his tee shot into the water and made double bogey. He then hooked his tee shot at the 18th into the water for another double bogey. The round spun away from him, and he needed back-to-back birdies to close to avoid shooting 80. Afterward, he was steaming. He was frustrated not just with his swing, which was ostensibly what he was working on as I watched him on the range. He was infuriated with how he handled the round with his brain.

"I was way more frustrated and upset with how I was mentally," Justin told the press the next day. "I felt like my course management was not strong," he said. " . . . I was two under, and I'd hit one green through seven holes. And then on seventeen I made the wrong decision. And then made the wrong decision off the tee on eighteen.

"That's the kind of stuff that pisses me off. If I manage everything well, even as bad as I hit it, I still feel like I could have gotten around in par."

So many elite athletes—shoot, so many weekend warriors—have experienced similar frustrations. Why didn't I play smarter? Why did I make such poor decisions? Why can't I recognize these situations in the moment and prevent bad situations from becoming worse?

The truth is that it's less important to *look back* on the what and the why, and more important to return to the present. Successful people not only maximize their opportunities. Successful people control and contain their setbacks.

This is true not only for Justin Thomas at the Players Championship—and we'll get to his response in a while. But it's also true for athletes—and professionals in any pursuit, regardless of the sport or business, irrespective of the circumstance and the adversity, whether they're on national television or working through private issues at home.

I always liken the pursuit of success to climbing Mt. Everest. You're going to slip. You're going to fall. You're going to plateau. You're going to need to rest, to get your breath back, to start again—only to fall and slip and go farther down than you were. Again, the whole idea is that progress isn't a straight line. I do believe there are athletes out there who understand that better than others, and who therefore have an ability to deal with that reality in a more successful way.

Some athletes feel the pain and can't absorb it or deal with it. They take a minor issue and make it a major hindrance. Other athletes deal with the pain in the moment and then quickly move on. Others don't feel that much pain from an individual setback because they have a deep understanding that there's a longer goal out there. They try to learn and grow, despite the obstacles and adversity, and know that they have to keep moving forward, trusting that they'll eventually see progress. And then there are others who are just totally in denial about the pain, people who keep going and are almost oblivious to the setback in the first place.

Take Shai Gilgeous-Alexander, the star of the Oklahoma City Thunder. (He's not a client, by the way. But he's an extremely public figure.) After winning his first NBA Most Valuable Player award following the 2024–25 season, he spoke about a book he had been given years earlier: *Zen in the Martial Arts* by Joe Hyams. In theory, it's about karate. But Gilgeous-Alexander—a player who was traded once on the night he was drafted, then after his rookie season—focused on the deeper theme.

"The message in the book was basically that success isn't linear. So it's never like this," he said during his acceptance speech as he moved his arm in a straight, upward trajectory. "It's always up and down, and you dip three to go up four, and then you dip again to go up six, and before you look at it, you're up ten. . . . Once I read that book, that's how I always looked at it. So if we were in a drought, or we're in a three-game losing streak—or at some point it was a seventeen-game losing streak . . . there's always a light at the end of the tunnel if you trust the work and you stick with it."

There are so many examples of this across sports, business, and life. When Boston Celtics star Jayson Tatum suffered a torn Achilles tendon in the 2025 playoffs—an injury that contributed to the Celtics' loss to the New York Knicks and could keep the five-time all-NBA player out for as long as a year—he almost immediately texted Reggie Miller, the Hall of Fame player and broadcaster: "This injury will not define me." That response shows that Tatum was dealing with his setback from a certain altitude. It cost him in the moment. It contributed to his team's demise that season. It wouldn't determine the overall arc of his career. I don't know Jayson Tatum, but I found that attitude—at what amounts to his lowest moment—impressive and even inspirational.

Listening to athletes who have endured such an array of setbacks can help us deal with our own. The number one thing we talk about doing in all of these situations: Reset. I've said it so many times already. I'll say it again because it's that important: Get back to the present.

In golf, you have way more time to reset than you do in basketball, where the play continues after you miss a layup, or even baseball, where the next pitch is coming quickly after you swung and missed. This is where deploying some of the tools you have filled your toolbox with can come in. Those tools—redoing the Velcro on your golf glove, repeating your goal words, resetting when your foot hits the tee box, whatever you choose—can help reset you in the present. In grounding yourself in the present, they can also help contain whatever setback just happened, be it a wayward tee shot or a double bogey.

Go back to Justin Thomas at the Players. Pros often head to the back section of the range at TPC Sawgrass if they want to be removed from the crowds—kind of out of sight, out of mind. After the first round of the Players, Justin wasn't really on anyone's mind. Three players shot 66 that day. Justin was a dozen shots back of them.

So how to deal with that setback? For Justin, hitting balls was part of the process of moving on. His performance off the tee and with his irons had been as bad as any round of the year. He knew it was an outlier, that one round of golf didn't represent the kind of golf he had been playing all season. "It was a fluke," he told reporters. But he also needed to cleanse it from his system. So in the heat of the Florida afternoon— I think it was like five hours—he not only hit balls, but he slammed his club at a bag of balls, signs of frustration I hadn't really seen from him.

Successful people often deal with setbacks. They also have to deal with success. In a now-famous speech he delivered at Dartmouth College in 2024, tennis legend Roger Federer imparted a great deal of wisdom on this subject.

*You can work harder than you thought possible and still lose. I have. In tennis, perfection is impossible. . . . In the*

*1,526 singles matches I played in my career, I won almost 80 percent of those matches. Now, I have a question for all of you: What percentage of the points do you think I won in those matches? Only 54 percent. In other words, even top-ranked tennis players win barely more than half of the points they play. When you lose every second point, on average, you learn not to dwell on every shot. . . .*

*The truth is, whatever game you play in life, sometimes you're going to lose. A point, a match, a season, a job. It's a roller coaster, with many ups and downs. And it's natural, when you're down, to doubt yourself. To feel sorry for yourself.*

*And by the way, your opponents have self-doubt, too. Don't ever forget that.*

*But negative energy is wasted energy. You want to become a master at overcoming hard moments. That to me is the sign of a champion.*

What an amazing glimpse into the mindset of a legend. Justin Thomas is an example of employing those thoughts. He rose to be the number one player in the world in 2018 and won two major championships. Those are the standards he set for himself. That's the level at which he expects to perform. Getting to the top of Mt. Everest may not be a linear process. Neither is getting back there again. Earning success doesn't often feel like an endpoint. Successful people often find themselves chasing success again.

For a football player, winning a Super Bowl is a lifelong dream. When the Philadelphia Eagles won in February

2025, Jalen Hurts, their star quarterback, summed it up like this: "The joy of winning it still had no comparison to the pain of losing it. And so those things are still going to continue to motivate me and drive me internally." A. J. Brown, their Pro Bowl receiver, described it this way: "I tried to feel how everybody made it seem to be a champion and unfortunately it was short-lived—two days to be exact. I've been a champion at the highest level before, but I thought my hard work would be justified by winning it all. It wasn't. My thrill for this game comes when I dominate. It's the hunt that does it for me."

Scottie Scheffler worked to become the top-ranked player in the world, and his run from 2022 to 2025—a run that may well keep going—is in discussion as the best sustained performance since Tiger Woods. As interesting as Scottie's golf is, his approach gained considerable attention in 2025, as he won both the PGA Championship and the Open Championship to get within one leg of the career Grand Slam. (It's important to note that I have never worked with Scottie.) Scheffler's pre-tournament thoughts about his approach to tournament golf in the days leading up to the Open at Royal Portrush garnered a lot of attention.

> *This is not a fulfilling life. It's fulfilling from the sense of accomplishment, but it's not fulfilling from a sense of the deepest places of your heart. . . . That's something that I wrestle with on a daily basis. It's like showing up at the Masters every year; it's like why do I want to win this golf tournament so badly? Why do I want to win the Open*

*Championship so badly? I don't know because, if I win, it's going to be awesome for two minutes. . . .*

*You win it, you celebrate, get to hug my family, my sister's there, it's such an amazing moment. Then it's like, "OK, what are we going to eat for dinner?" Life goes on. It feels like you work your whole life to celebrate winning a tournament for like a few minutes. It only lasts a few minutes. . . .*

*We work so hard for such little moments. I'm kind of sicko. I love putting in the work, I love getting to practice, I love getting to live out my dreams. But at the end of the day, sometimes I just don't understand the point.*

There's a lot of truth, and some real lessons, in there. In some corners, Scheffler was misinterpreted. Did he mean he didn't *care* about golf? No, not at all. He meant he wouldn't be defined by his results, and that his deepest fulfillment actually comes from other areas of his life. He was only twenty-nine when he uttered those words. They're full of real wisdom.

I think of it like a band that records a debut album that climbs to the top of the charts. If the band responds to that success by chasing the next number one record, it's not being true to the reasons it produced the hot record in the first place. If a major winner chases the next major, he's not staying present in the methods and practices that led to the first major. We see it all the time. The guys who are ranked in the top ten in the world want to stay in the top ten, and when they fall out, they're desperate to get back there. Bring that same philosophy to your local club or muni: A player who was a single-digit handicapper and now plays to a 12 wants to get back to where she was—or better.

Part of dealing with success is somehow allowing it not to define you. A Masters champion will always be a Masters champion, whether he wins another Masters or not. (He has a dinner invitation for a Tuesday night in April, along with a green jacket, to prove it.) The number one player in the world may or may not become number one again. If a setback can't be defining, then neither can a high point. There must be meaning, purpose—and joy—in the process and the pursuit.

I know an owner of a sports franchise who has relentlessly chased building the best team possible. He wants to win championships badly. His life will not be different from the money he will make if they win, or the praise for his organization. His energy is focused on building a team. He loves the opportunity to create chemistry and trusts that with the right chemistry, good things will happen. His focus is clearly on the process of building excellence. Sure, the reward for his efforts is certainly enhanced if his team wins. He smiles and celebrates more. But if he only allowed himself to be joyful if he won the championship, he would be miserable most seasons. The odds of winning a championship every year don't exist. He isn't fazed by those odds. I don't even think he cares about those odds. His joy is in the vision he has for the culture he is building and the team he is assembling. He believes the payoff will come if he stays focused on the process.

Many of us work at difficult jobs, where the process is

tedious and the successes can be hard to appreciate. A salesperson can take months to complete a deal. Manufacturing jobs can be limited to installing one piece into a car, and the workers don't get to see—and appreciate—the finished product. Writing a book is an arduous (though, at times, enjoyable) task, and I keep trying to put my thoughts out in the best way I can. There are countless jobs where people watch the clock and work till they are told they can stop and go home. How do those hardworking folks define success?

Many people are able to see their jobs merely as a vehicle to provide the kind of life they want to live, and how they live that life is actually a better marker of success. Which is an important concept: Success is ultimately defined by the individual on her or his own personal terms. We each have to define what we want to be visible. What are the primary qualities we want to live with and the rules we want to live by? Success is ultimately defined by the individual on their own personal terms. Then happiness—and, in turn, success—are a result of the enrichment in our lives that those qualities bring us.

Arthur Brooks is a well-respected teacher in the Harvard Business School. He has held disparate jobs such as playing the French horn in symphonies and being head of a moderate-right-wing think tank. He writes about happiness and goals in his books frequently. One central idea: "The key to happiness is not being rich; it's doing something arduous and creating something of value and then being able to reflect on the fruits of your labor."

Let's go back to where this chapter started, with Justin

Thomas. All successful golfers have to know how to bounce back from setbacks. Justin has done it in ways both big and small. At the 2022 PGA Championship, he began the third round in third place, shot 4-over par to fall seven shots back, then bogeyed the third hole of the final round to sink eight shots behind. But he stayed focused, shot a gritty 67 on Sunday to force a playoff, then beat Will Zalatoris. The setback of Saturday didn't define his Sunday.

"A lot of self-belief, a lot of patience," he said of how he hung in there. "I wasn't looking at leaderboards today. I was just trying to play golf."

Setbacks can feel different depending on how we felt our effort was on a given day or in a given round. For all the things we can't control in golf, we can control our effort. If we try our best, what more can we ask of ourselves? What more can anyone ask of us? But processing setbacks or losses also involves patience. We have all recalled a drive home after a tournament or a match that we lost—or even if we just played poorly. Those losses don't sit well with a lot of us. They can be frustrating.

But at some point, those losses transition into preparation for the next time out. That's what Justin did at the 2022 PGA Championship (which, to be clear, came before I began working with him). Processing the setback properly can involve so many tools in our toolbox. Journaling can be effective. Meditating works for lots of people. Breathing exercises are tremendous. Some athletes find going to church to be their best way to reset. All of those methods incorporate patience, and it's worth noting that there is great skill in having patience and knowing when and how to use it. There is patience in realizing the good will eventually outweigh the bad. There is patience in understanding that the poor lie that resulted from an errant drive is an opportunity with the next shot. Patience is a function of self-esteem, of trust in yourself, and it's essential in recovering from a setback.

There is also patience in forgiving yourself. That could be for a loss or a poor performance. This goes back to the negative voices and scarring experiences we might have from our past that cause us to carry judgments about ourselves when we lose. Failure can make those feelings surface and become more acute. It's exactly at that moment of self-loathing after a loss when forgiveness becomes essential. We have to realize: We all lose. It's part of competition. It's part of life.

Basketball Hall of Famer Kareem Abdul-Jabbar put it this way: "You can't win until you learn to lose." Bart Giamatti, the late commissioner of Major League Baseball, described his sport not in the rosiest of terms, but in a way that makes it real: "It breaks your heart. It is designed to break your heart. The game begins in spring, when everything else begins again, and it blossoms in summer, filling the afternoons and evenings, and then as soon as the chill rains come, it stops and leaves you to face the fall alone."

You can't have victory without a loser, and my players all have to come to terms with the idea that losing is part of every competition. Think of a full-field PGA Tour event with 156 players. There's only one winner. Are the other 155 losers? If any of those players feel like their performance that week was a setback, they must bring patience to the situation, accept the result, forgive themselves for whatever went wrong, recover and stride forward with self-belief.

Even at the end of a miserable day at the Players, Justin Thomas knew he wasn't the kind of player who turns in 78s and is closer to the last player in the field than the top of the board. The setback was temporary. One thing we remind each other of often is: Talent never goes away. Some of the peripheries around talent—diligence, focus, commitment, etc.—can ebb and flow. Other thoughts can enter the head. But the talent is always there. You just have to figure out how to access it.

For Justin, accessing the talent meant swinging more freely without fear of the outcome. The next day in the second round at TPC Sawgrass, after spending the previous evening beating balls on the range for hours to reset his mind, he piped his first drive down the middle of the fairway, hit his approach to six feet, and rolled in the putt for the first of five birdies on the front nine. By the time he got to the 18th tee, he had made six more birdies on the back, was 11 under for the day, and was on pace to set a new course record. After all those hours on the range, had he fixed something in his swing? No, he had fixed something in his mind.

"Mentally was the biggest thing," he told reporters afterward. "I felt like I did an unbelievable job of just staying— keeping my eyes forward, keeping my blinders on, not looking backwards, forwards or anything like that. It was just, 'How can I put this ball in the fairway off the tee? And then how can I make birdie? And let's rinse and repeat.'"

Talent hadn't gone away. It was right there, waiting to be

accessed. Yes, he bogeyed 18 that day—the little step back on the route up Everest—but he finished with a 62 that tied the course record.

"One of the best rounds I've played, for sure," he said afterward. One of the best rounds from a guy who has played a lot of fantastic rounds—all some 24 hours after one of his worst rounds. Because he didn't chase success. Because he reset. Because the talent was still in there. It all meant he could minimize his setback, which is one of the building blocks for success.

Chapter 11

# Pressure and Confidence

*"Pressure is a privilege. It only comes to those who earn it."*
—Billie Jean King

O ne of my clients worked his way into contention at an early-season tournament during the PGA Tour's West Coast swing. As he reached the back nine in Sunday's final round, the stakes grew higher, and he slowed down—noticeably. This player typically takes 10 to 12 seconds behind and over the ball before he unleashes his swing. Here, with the pressure of the tournament clearly entering his mind, he was taking twice as long—20 to 24 seconds over the ball. And he's not a slow player. He just hates slow play.

When this player was playing his best golf—which wasn't during the few months that led to this particular Sunday in February—he never worried that a putt wasn't going to go in. He never played defensively. His last thought before he hit a shot was never, "Uh-oh. There's trouble left. I better not hit it left." It was always to pick his intended target and swing freely toward it. He had learned and employed the kind of thinking we talk about all the time: We always want the last thought in our minds to be about where we want to hit the ball instead of where we don't.

By the time he reached the back nine on Sunday, he had lost that intentional focus and feeling. On Saturday, he had birdied the ninth hole. On Sunday, he didn't—and he immediately felt like he had to make up for it by birdieing 10. That kind of thinking introduces pressure. In so many ways, he was changing his behavior and mindset to fit this specific situation, rather than repeating the behaviors that had put him in contention in the first place.

We all do this. Pressure isn't reserved for the final nine holes of a PGA Tour event. It can come when you're one up on your friend in a $10 Nassau, and the tee shot at 18 awaits. It can be self-induced, when you just made double bogey at 17 and now need to par 18 to break 80. Different circumstances affect all of us differently.

That same player who played decidedly slower with the tournament on the line told me that when he plays in social events or matches—even if they're televised, even if people are watching from the gallery—he handles his game and himself so much better. He's more relaxed, able to stay present, and much more committed to his process than his results. In those situations, it's not about climbing to the No. 1 ranking in the world. It's not about taking home the millions of dollars that would be the winner's share of the purse. It's not about legacy. It's about competition. For him, it's freeing. He's focused, yet not tense.

Competitive, but not frustrated. Why is this? How do we find that sweet spot between focused intention and still playing with freedom and joy?

Another client is an executive at a Fortune 500 company. She's an absolute rock star in her world. She regularly addresses packed convention halls. She's an incredible and inspiring leader. In this Silicon Valley environment—decked out in a Chanel suit, behind a microphone and a lectern, looking out at ten thousand people who have signed up to see her and listen to her and receive her message—she is confident. She gets standing ovations. She is present and intentional. She delivers.

Put this superstar executive in a small group, though, and her confidence wavers. She can hear her voice crack. Her hands tremble slightly when she reaches for a sip of water. She doesn't deliver her message as forcefully. She tries to impress her colleagues with jokes. Looking those colleagues in the eye, one by one, is somehow different from staring into a sea of nameless, faceless conventioneers. It's personal. She finds it hard. And she abandons the qualities that put her there in the first place.

There's a connection between these two—the golfer on the back nine in contention, and the exec in the small meeting. The best-selling author Marianne Williamson has a quote that applies:

*Our deepest fear is not that we are inadequate. Our deepest fear is that we are powerful beyond measure. It is our light, not our darkness, that most frightens us.*

We often talk about fear of failure. But what my two clients were experiencing in different places, and what Williamson is pointing out here, is that our greater fear can actually be of success. Can I live up to the expectations of others? Can I live up to the talents and qualities that I truly believe I have somewhere inside me? Can I allow myself to have beautiful things? Think about areas of your own life where that might apply. That could easily be on the golf course. But we could also find ourselves afraid of taking the steps we need to be successful at home or at work.

I call this kind of thinking "success consciousness," and we can find examples of it all over. I was once on a panel with the owner of a Super Bowl–winning NFL franchise who was asked a simple question: How did you ever get the idea of buying a football team? He was surprised at the question. He was bewildered by the notion that he wouldn't allow himself to attain his dream. Yes, he had resources that made his dream possible, but it was his belief in the power and intention of these dreams that really led to him pulling it off. Discipline and hard work can help all of us achieve as much as we can, yet believing you are deserving of success is where the "success consciousness" fits in. Once we *believe* we deserve success then we can create a plan and intentions to manifest our dreams. Can I break 80 this summer? Can I win the club championship? Can I create a successful start-up—believing in my product and my people so completely that I raise all the necessary funds?

These ideas of handling pressure and believing we are deserving of success even come up in the popular world of You-

Tube golf. Grant Horvat is a star in that world. There's not a shot he can't hit, and his videos can be mesmerizing. He has a regular bit where he challenges tour pros—the best players in the world—to matches in which he gets a five-stroke advantage.

Phil Mickelson—who spent some time wondering why Horvat got a five-shot advantage over Jon Rahm but wasn't whittling that down for a fifty-something Phil—asked Horvat as they rode in the cart between shots of their match why he didn't push himself to qualify for the highest levels of the game. It's a reasonable question given Horvat's obvious talent. Horvat talked about his time playing college golf.

"I don't love super-competitive golf," Horvat said. "When I get in tournaments, you get down on yourself. It's mental warfare out there. So, I just didn't enjoy that mental warfare. I would rather come out here and do this. I love competing. Don't get me wrong. I'm very competitive. I want to beat you really bad right now.

"But in a tournament, I get really tense, and I start trying to guide it and everything. On YouTube, it's just like—I'm sending it."

How do we access that mentality—just send it—even when there's obvious pressure? The stakes might be different for Horvat, because his goal of becoming a YouTube star is so different from being a top-10 player on the PGA Tour. It's not about world ranking and money lists and more about pure entertainment. Yet this question applies to the golf course and the boardroom, and it applies to Horvat's YouTube videos because he now has a product people like and a standard to uphold. How do we relax and reach our most comfortable mindset when the stakes are high? Our best characteristics can feel unavailable at those crucial points. How do we access them when we need them?

First, I don't like to think of these situations as *issues* or *problems.* Let's reframe them as *opportunities.* In talking with both the golfer who slowed down on the back nine and the exec who struggled in an intimate setting, the solutions are remarkably similar. The golfer was aware he was slowing down under pressure, and he wanted to change that. The executive knew that she was visibly nervous in front of small groups, and she wanted to improve. Each had achieved the first step: Acknowledge and become aware of what is happening. Remember the Socrates quote? "An unexamined life is not worth living"? Examine yourself.

In any situation involving pressure, there is noise in our heads. It doesn't matter if the pressure is perceived or real; our bodies can't tell the difference. Pushing back on the noise, trying to force it to be quiet, can exacerbate the problem. Plus, trying to suppress the noise can identify it as a negative development, which can make us feel worse. I find the best advice is to simply acknowledge that the noise is there. Kobe Bryant frequently spoke about the way he handled and trained for pressure.

"Pressure does not exist. It is in the imagination," he said in an interview with the author Jay Shetty. "We create pressure ourselves. . . . If you're afraid to fail, then you are probably going to fail."

Bryant developed his own philosophy he famously labeled the "Mamba Mentality": "It means to be constantly trying to be the best version of yourself." In his book of the same name, he continued:

*I never felt outside pressure. I knew what I wanted to accomplish, and I knew how much work it took to achieve those goals. I then put in the work and trusted in it. Besides, the expectations I placed on myself were higher than what anyone expected from me. . . . A big shot is just another shot. People make a huge deal out of clutch shots. Thing is, it's just one shot. If you make a thousand shots a day, it's just one of a thousand. Once you're hitting that many, what's one more? That was my mentality from day one.*

Kobe was very tuned to his inner world. He recognized each moment and its meaning and didn't try to make a big situation smaller. He embraced it and trained for it. We can all learn from that mindset.

*It's the back nine on Sunday. I'm in contention in the tournament. I'm slowing down my pre-shot routine. I can acknowledge that is happening. I know I'm supposed to keep close to the same time over the ball regardless of the situation. Let's get back to that.*

Or . . .

*I'm in a small-group meeting. My hands are shaking a little bit. I'm not speaking as clearly or confidently as I want. It's good to be aware of all that is happening and what I'm feeling inside.*

This is part of mindfulness, of awareness, and it can be one of the main goals of meditation, as we have discussed.

This is a way that the tenets practiced in meditation can translate to the course or the boardroom. There's no reason to judge the noise. Just observe it. Over time, the noise that enters our head can simply become a sound that we recognize. It's less a distraction, and more just a state of being. The noise then loses its power over us and becomes much more manageable.

If either my golfer or my executive can apply these tools when they're back in those situations, they can feel more in control of the noise and create the environment that they want. This way the pressure doesn't weigh on them as much. It doesn't create a negative tailspin. It's acknowledged. The mere awareness serves to remind us to get back to how we want to feel. Each of them can go on and perform, whether that's executing a free swing or solving problems through clear communication and decisive thinking, while delivering a message with confidence and self-belief. We let go of the fear of being successful and instead embrace the behaviors that brought out our best performances.

Some of the noise that gets in our heads and affects our performance can be traced to the actual situation. But I believe—and I work with my clients on this—that to truly quiet the noise, we must get in touch with what's going on internally. What could be bothering us at home that we're bringing to the golf course? What relationship issue could be disrupting our work? Are we feeling like other issues at home or in life are intruding on our performance—be it in golf or in our professional lives?

Two leading psychologists have complementary views on

understanding confidence. Carol Dweck has done foundational work establishing that it's helpful to have a mindset of growth rather than a fixed perspective. The fixed mindset maintains that abilities are static, that they don't change, that they're almost permanent. The growth mindset emphasizes the capacity to develop and learn. The attributes of the growth mindset are resilience and learning through experience, with an underlying faith that this learning is beneficial. If you have a growth mindset, you'll apply what you're learning to your craft.

The other psychologist, Martin Seligman, explains how attitudes will influence how we learn and how we can envision our future. He describes how through evolution in prehistoric times, a pessimistic style that preached caution and care helped protect us. The idea: We were careful because we didn't want to be eaten by saber-toothed cats! Seligman studied the ways people learned to do new tasks and found that about one-third of his subjects would continue to pursue learning even if the tasks became difficult. The pessimists viewed their difficulties as their limitations. They were stuck. Optimists saw their failures as small and temporary.

This directly relates to my career and to some of my most successful players on tour. There are moments when even the best golfers can live in both the pessimistic and optimistic worlds. They may feel hopeless and doomed, but they are determined to find a better way. They prepare and practice before the actual event. Just like hitting wedge shots on the range, we can practice our mental tools and strategies.

I work with a player who was in that discussion no PGA

Tour golfer wants to be in: one of the best players who had never won a major. He was viewed by the press as doomed. In one sense, he lived in a shadow of never achieving his potential. On the other hand, he never lost belief in his ability. He struggled to focus that ability to hit the right shot in key moments. Standing over a ball, he had racing thoughts of how to hit a particular shot and all the things that could go wrong. Physically, he had all the tools to be confident in his game. Mentally, he couldn't control his mind to put that confidence into play.

So we went to work. We worked hard for two years to transition from his overall confidence in shot-making to specifics on how to maximize his results. He loved risk and yet had a keen sense of the probability of pulling off each shot. He knew which shots were risky. Our work was to maximize risk/reward and avoid mistakes. This mainly involved visualizing his shots and using his creativity to choose the proper shot in a particular circumstance. In competition, he had to learn how to slow his thoughts down, while keeping his pre-shot routine relatively the same. He worked diligently on these mental strategies at home—meditation, goal-setting, therapy—to know himself on and off the course. He went on to win three times—including a breakthrough in a major—after a few years working together.

I believe some of that success happened because he learned to be confident and control his thinking during competition. He became more intentional and less skittish. He started to enjoy the challenges of individual shots and slowed the game down enough to trust that every shot was something that he had practiced before. He went back to Kobe's work on Mamba Mentality. He was excited to hit a shot in front of millions of people that he had already hit in his mind on the range.

Another of my players would always slouch when he walked in between shots. He would droop his shoulders and curve his back forward as he walked down the fairway. He not only didn't look confident. He wasn't confident. We worked on helping him feel strong in his body, to stride purposefully and stand tall. Our gait can reflect the way we feel and think.

Think about that when you hit a poor shot. How are you carrying yourself, and what does that say about your ability to be in the proper frame of mind for the next shot? With this player, I even applied a piece of black tape on the back of his shirt that would pucker if his shoulders fell in disappointment or frustration. It sent him a signal that his posture had fallen, which meant his mind was off course, too. As he began to feel better about himself, he started to walk differently. This was less about golf itself and all about his view of himself and living in the world. Walk like a champion, feel like a champion.

We should all do that consciously. Bring your energy, strength, and optimism to all of the things that challenge you. But it has to be sincere, and not an empty attitude. With one of my players, we continually worked to temper his optimism with analytics to create the optimal risk-adjusted approach. He was very confident and optimistic—to a fault, actually. He would find a tiny hole through branches and think, "I could hit it through there." We've all done something like that.

Eventually, though, he realized that he had to merge these two qualities—his golf IQ, and his newly discovered emotional intelligence (EQ). He had to channel his abilities to express his creativity and to navigate the course efficiently. He replaced the excitement of hitting individual shots that might carry with them a high amount of risk with a more methodical plan that would help him win. He used a data analyst—who happened to be a reformed gambler, so he knew something about risk/reward—to help him understand the stats of every hole on a course. He figured out the positions from which the most birdies or eagles were made on each hole. He began to trust that he could win through blending his talents rather than maximizing separate skills. The sum was greater than the individual parts. And while we all can't hire people to dissect the courses we play, we can certainly work on merging our course management with an understanding of how and why we feel the way we do. It is as simple as using your heart and mind together.

Another example: I had a college player who had a low threshold for frustration and anger. He was gifted, but he couldn't tolerate poor shots. He would become tense and distraught after even a small failure. He held a combination of mindsets—both growth and pessimistic—and he struggled to stay in a more productive growth mindset. He had endured significant losses in his life. As a result, the ability to believe that everything would be okay had escaped him. We worked hard to help him see how his past losses had influenced his ability to maintain his growth mindset. He started to see his failures as a way to learn how to compose himself in competition. Think about that: Mistakes eventually became lessons, and lessons became achievements. That's growth.

This player developed a belief that he could take the same failure and make it a learning opportunity. Eventually, he learned to prefer the teachable moments to grow from his mistakes. As the cost of his own errors decreased, he was freer and able to bring out his best version of himself. This is the definition of using failure as an opportunity. And it's a way for us all to maintain confidence.

One more example: I worked with an executive who was one step removed from his dream job. He wanted to be in the C-suite, and he wanted to be senior management. He felt talented and smart and had been successful in his business dealings. He worked for an investment firm and had made successful recommendations about financial opportunities and had helped the company flourish. Despite his successes, he wasn't given the chance to become a member of the senior leadership team. He was frustrated and felt belittled when opportunities to join the top level of executives would become available and he would be ignored. He had great confidence in his analytic abilities and thought that would be enough to gain him entrance to management.

Despite our efforts, he couldn't look at his interpersonal relationships with other members of his team. He had a growth mindset in one sector of his mind—objective success—but didn't pay attention to the mindset of being a teacher and a leader. He had trouble listening and receiving feedback and often was defensive at his year-end reviews. Consequently, even with considerable discourse, he never understood what was holding him back. The key reason: his inability to observe himself and to recognize his growth areas and use that as motivation. He could not get past his bitterness when he wasn't promoted. He was unwilling or unable to take responsibility for his own mistakes. It was sad to watch. He was often very good at his job and helped his investment firm make loads of money. However, his emotional intelligence never matched up with his technical skills. I watched him leave the company while blaming his supervisors for their unfair evaluations of his work. Emotional intelligence demands honesty and self-reflection. If you cannot see reality, you won't change yourself.

Go back to my two clients from the start of this chapter— the golfer struggling with his routine in the pressure of a tournament and the executive worried about her performance in smaller groups. Each was having trouble accessing the best versions of themselves when they needed it most. And it's because each was changing their behavior to match the moment and maybe overly reading the environment. They both failed at understanding how to read themselves, rather than the world around them. The golfer took longer—too long— over a shot, when he had put himself in that very position after hitting the shot using his normal pre-shot routine and not getting stuck in his thoughts. His talent and work ethic should be enough. Some of my clients will question their ability to hit certain shots at key moments in competition after having successfully hit the same shots in practice repeatedly. They can hit a 4-iron 220 yards with a five-foot draw ten consecutive times, with the exact same swing speed and direction. Yet even as they're doing that on the range, they question whether they'll be able to hit the exact same shot on the course. The executive had risen through the ranks of her company based on her skill and judgment, yet she was often forced to pause and doubt her abilities.

Examples of these struggles with confidence under pressure are almost too many to count—which is one reason none of us should worry about acknowledging our own issues at crucial junctures. I have an LPGA player who is obsessed with the mechanics of her body, her ability to turn and move the way she wants. I have another player who becomes obsessed with his technique and swing plane and hounds his coach to help him find the proper approach thirty minutes before his tee time. I have an executive who is constantly second-guessing her decisions and pondering the alternative choices she might have made in the small group. I have another executive who thought she had to be funny and caring to hook the people in her meeting when her ideas on their own were brilliant. Her intellect had put her in position to lead the meeting in the first place. Yet her self-doubt always reappeared.

To heal these issues, each golfer or businessperson has to reach a better understanding of her own emotions and behaviors. Those moments of doubt are the wake-up calls for each of my clients. It is the moment when they look inside and trust who they are and what they can do. Eleanor Roosevelt said, "No one can make you feel inferior without your own consent." Only when you understand that can your confidence return when you need it. Only then can you pull off the shot that's required with the tournament on the line using the routines that created all the previous shots. Only then can you conduct the meeting by leaning on your own ideas. Pressure should bring out our confidence, not inhibit it.

# Chapter 12

# Stigma

*"It's okay to not be okay, and it's okay to talk about it."*
—Naomi Osaka

Not long ago, I attended a wedding with a mixed crowd—a crossover of people I know from my personal and professional lives. Also in attendance were a few high-ranking officials from the PGA Tour, mostly people I know in passing rather than in-depth.

Over the course of the evening, I fell into conversation with one of those high-ranking officials. Mental health is such an important aspect of all of our lives, and it's in the midst of a multi-year moment in sports. Prominent international athletes from gymnast Simone Biles to swimmer Michael Phelps to tennis champion Naomi Osaka have all addressed mental well-being in different, public, and important ways. In my view, the PGA Tour lags behind. With a top decision-maker right in front of me, I decided to go for it.

I pointed out to the official that at every PGA Tour stop, there's a physical therapy trailer. There are equipment trailers. There's a workout trailer. There's this trailer, that trailer, trailers all over the place.

Why not have a mental health trailer?

"I've heard that idea from a few people," the official said. "The problem is: Who will let themselves be seen walking in there?"

I was astonished. I was also disappointed. Since I first began working with both men and women professional golfers over a quarter century ago, the message has gotten louder but not much has actually changed. We have come so far in being more open about mental health—both in society at large and, slowly, in professional golf. Many athletes from a range of different sports speak openly about their challenges while inspiring others to not be embarrassed or feel shame around their struggles. Documentaries have been made explaining the many mental health challenges we all may go through specifically with competitive athletes as well as musicians. Books and Instagram posts explain these struggles as well as giving tips of different tools to use to address them including a myriad of treatment modalities ranging from psychodynamic theory to the use of psychedelics in the treatment of post-traumatic stress disorder.

Yet the story above speaks to the stigma that still exists. It's a stigma we all have to move beyond if we're going to truly take care of ourselves, be healthy, and grow. The people at the top levels of the PGA Tour wouldn't support a mental health trailer because they thought players would be too embarrassed to use it? That's wild. Life on tour is inherently isolating. Golf, as a sport, is incredibly tough mentally. There are no teammates with whom to share blame. Performance and results are up to the individual. We should be encouraging players to tend to their mental health, not running from it because we assume they wouldn't want to be seen as weak or soft, just as any of us in any walk of life should have no issues admitting we're tending to our mental health by meditating or talking to a therapist. The tour was rocked by the death of Grayson Murray, a well-respected player, amazing and thoughtful man, and tour winner in the same year that he took his own life. Players admired him. Some knew of his struggles. Most, however, couldn't have been aware of how much he was actually suffering.

The isolation of depression, anxiety, and the subsequent development of addiction can be crippling for so many of us. Depression and isolation often can be a significant struggle for those in the entertainment industry as well, as they attempt to keep a game face, an ironic phrase for sports, entertainment, and life itself. In Grayson's case, the loss and grieving led to some begrudging recognition of the stress inherent in competing in golf. Because Grayson's parents have been open about their son's struggles and the pain they live with every day, there have been more discussions and gatherings of souls that have lived through loss. But in reality, none of that led to meaningful action across the PGA Tour. There have been no surveys of the entire tour to assess the prevalence of mood disorders in players. There has been no widespread acknowledgment of the mental challenges inherent in competitive golf and how the tour might best help the people who make their product. At a moment when other sports and prominent athletes are making sure mental health is a priority, the world of professional golf is mostly shrugging it off or giving it lip service.

There is more attention on the PGA Tour to physical therapy and physical recovery than mental therapy and mental recovery. None of the spaces mentioned above—spaces the tour offers for physical therapy, conditioning, and recovery—encompass mental wellness, talk therapy, or even contact numbers for players, families, volunteers, or employees who might have immediate concerns or be approaching a crisis. This is such a missed opportunity, almost an antiquated approach, and it's something those of us who run businesses should be conscious of as we take care of our employees.

I have thought so much about this. There are so many ideas about how the tour and the sport could improve. At each tournament site, there could be headphones and apps for biofeedback devices and Apple watches to track heart rate, blood pressure, or even heart-rate variability—that newer diagnostic tool that can measure physiological stress we discussed earlier. There are many healing modalities available to attain more relaxed states. Many players wear these devices routinely when they play—a ring or wristband to measure a broad array of physiological parameters, which can in turn help them learn to better control their emotions. They're not a bad idea for any of us who want to be more conscious about tracking the relationship between our physical and mental states.

But there's so much more. The professional golf tours

could create sanctuary spaces to meditate, decompress, or simply sit on a beanbag chair and get out of the heat with their peers. There could be both saunas and cold plunge tubs for use in recovery, both physical and physiological healing that could be freely available and integrated into places where meditation or therapy could be provided. I believe it's time to make mental health and recovery equal to physical health and recovery. That should become the standard way to think for all athletes—not to mention the rest of us—and it should be encouraged and supported by the leagues that make their money off those athletes.

Even after some time and distance from the moment, I'm still surprised by the tour official's response: Who would be seen going into a mental health trailer? Like, that would be embarrassing? That's almost Cro-Magnon in its thinking.

Yet if we go back to earlier in my career—not that long ago, to be honest—examples of an overwhelming reluctance to admit mental health challenges were all over the place. I had so many clients who didn't even want to be seen with me at the golf course, so we would do all of our work by phone. This is still true for some players today, but the pendulum has finally started to swing. Even if players don't want to talk publicly about our work, it's much rarer for an athlete to be reluctant to acknowledge he's seeking help to work on his mental game. It's no longer seen as a weakness. It's seen as an advantage.

Even though I believe pro golf has a long way to go in that regard, it's instructive to see how far we have come. Earlier in my career, I had a client I had been working with behind the scenes for many years. This was back when my nickname actually was "Stealth," because so many caddies and agents knew I was working with players, but golf fans knew nothing about any of it. We were at a U.S. Open, one of the biggest stages in the sport. The tour player asked me to walk a practice round with him—something I do all the time. I was surprised that this player was comfortable enough with our work and his journey to be in public with me and even be seen with his mental coach.

I waited for him and his playing partners on the first tee at the famous Bethpage Black Golf Course in New York. When he arrived, he slipped under the ropes and offered his hand. "Hi," he said to me, looking me straight in the eye, "I'm Brian" (not his real name), and introduced himself to me. My fellow PGA Tour clients who either saw this or have heard about it have nicknamed Brian "Starbucks," because that's where we actually met—not on the golf course.

It seems funny to me now. He wanted me there to see how he worked and plotted around the course but wasn't willing to acknowledge I was there to work with him. That kind of stuff used to happen all the time. Yes, it has diminished. But it has hardly gone away.

It took time for many of my clients to embrace the idea not only that working with me was okay, but that *talking* about working with me was okay, too. Part of that reluctance is embedded in the mindset of athletes. Yet part of it is still because of the "kind" of work I'm known for, the "digging deep" aspect.

One player once said to me, "You do marriage counseling, right?" If that's the case, then to be seen walking or working with me would be an acknowledgment that a player's marriage might be in trouble. Well, I do some marriage counseling if I think it might help. But there shouldn't be a stigma about that, either. The heavier inner work is important, especially as it relates to our relationships with our families and friends. The stigma that needing mental or emotional support is a sign of weakness is damning for the players. It makes it harder for them to access help.

This stigma can also be reinforced by family members who are nervous about what will come out of my working with their husband or son. They can fear that talking through problems would actually wreck the player's world and shatter their friendships or marriage. Sometimes, they like the old version of their partner or family member and feel undermined when the new version creates new demands based on their own growth. Fortunately, by now, families who think this way are more in the minority. Most families of players welcome the support and insights that come from our work, and they understand that work provides hope that a player can become more well adjusted, which can translate into being a better father, husband, son, friend—and golfer.

The thirteenth-century poet, scholar, and mystic Rumi wrote: "The wound is the place where the light enters you." The late songwriter and poet Leonard Cohen put it this way: "There is a crack, a crack in everything. That's how the light gets in." Those words resonate now, in pro golf and in life. Acknowledge and explore the source of pain or problems, and then you can heal. We shouldn't run or hide from that process. We should embrace it.

J. B. Holmes was one of my first clients to "come out" about the value of taking care of your mental health so you can perform better. Coming out is kind of a ridiculous term, but it applies. J.B. began talking publicly about our work around the 2008 Ryder Cup in his native Kentucky. That's a good *decade* after I started working with PGA Tour players.

"I had been struggling on the course, thinking too much, maybe just worrying about stuff too much," J.B. said. "It's really helped to have [Julie's] experience, as long as she's been out here on tour, just talking to me, helping me being able to learn to control my thoughts a little better and be able to calm down. Once you clear your mind of some of that, you can focus better. It helps to know that you're not the only one dealing with that stuff."

Part of my goal in doing my work—and, indeed, in writing this book—is to make statements like J.B.'s above more of the norm, to push the idea that taking care of our mental health should be a common part of our weeks and our days. With all of us. Unfortunately, there are still so many pockets of resistance.

Many professional sports teams now employ a psychologist or mental health professional. They are required for NBA franchises. Hopefully this will quickly cross over to all sports. Yet the transition to more acceptance often suffers the same growing pains we have discussed in golf. Major League Baseball has significant player development programs that encompass life skills and baseball skills. There are great differences within these programs, however, regarding mental health development, social skills, and avoiding addiction. Many teams make real investments into the mental and emotional health of their players, but this effort isn't consistent across an entire league. Plus, I have had clients in team sports who are reluctant to work with a mental health professional who is employed by the team. There are trust issues. *Is this person just going to tell the front office what I'm going through?*

Not long ago, I walked with a client's group for the first two days of a tournament. In that group there was another player who I have known for years but never worked with. The player's wife asked me to work with them. Separately, the player's parents told me they were desperate for me to work with their son. The PGA Tour player said, "No," quickly and flatly. He simply doesn't think any issues he has at home, with his family, or in his relationships are having any impact on his golf. In my opinion, there's no way they're not. But this player was clearly worried about how working on his problems would be perceived.

Not everyone is ready to do the work, and so often the reason dates back to some old social norms. So many strong, amazing, accomplished athletes kind of believe that admitting to problems at home or in their relationships or even with their confidence shows weakness. But for me, it's the exact opposite. I hope tending to your mental health by talking with someone (in confidentiality) is a way of acknowledging that we all go through some versions of the same thing. We want to support a humility in ourselves that acknowledges that we don't understand everything about who we are, and that we often act unconsciously. As we know by now, Brené Brown writes frequently about the strength and creativity inherent in vulnerability. "Vulnerability," she wrote, "is not winning or losing; it's having the courage to show up and be seen when we have no control over the outcome."

There should be no distinction between the importance of our physical health and our mental health. There has never been shame in talking about the need to work out, to eat right, to take care of our bodies. Or a diagnosis of diabetes or rheumatoid arthritis. You wouldn't judge a person for getting treatment for a physical illness. But we should also acknowledge that exercising can have a positive impact on our mental health. People feel way better. Endorphins pump through their bodies. They have more self-esteem. Their outlook becomes more positive. That's huge.

Athletes can play a key role in destigmatizing mental health and performance. Phelps, the record-setting Olympic swimmer, has been quite open about his struggle with depression. "My depression and my anxiety is never going to just disappear," he told the website Healthline. "I'm never going to be able to snap my fingers and say 'Go away. Leave me alone.' It makes me. It is a part of me. It's always going to be a part of me."

Athletes coming forward to talk about their mental health can also have a huge impact on kids. Role models matter, and if a young golfer were to hear the best players in the world talking about how they tend to their minds, it might sow a seed at a young age. This is an accomplishment, but in my view, we need to do much more. A Johns Hopkins All Children's Hospital paper referenced a study that hospital visits for eating disorders by patients under the age of seventeen more than doubled between 2018 and 2022. The trappings of social media are perilous and omnipresent. We teach sexual education in middle school. Shouldn't we talk to kids who are eight, ten, or twelve about their mental health? Shouldn't we provide teenagers with tools to deal with the onslaught of pressures they face in a digital twenty-first century?

In the NFL playoffs, Philadelphia Eagles receiver A. J. Brown was shown during the broadcast reading a book on the bench in the middle of a game against the Green Bay Packers. The initial, off-the-cuff, external assessment was that Brown was blowing off his teammates and not focusing during the most important part of the season. What he was actually doing was reading a book called *Inner Excellence*, a tool he used to get him refocused between drives.

Here was a star player on the eventual Super Bowl champion tending to his mental health on national television in the middle of a game. The moment went viral. This was a player who carried a prior reputation as a diva, a prima donna. His time at the Eagles revealed a more complex picture of an individual who totally identified himself as a teammate while performing his job as an elite receiver. He was doing his inner work to influence his outer work. My hope is that the discourse changed, and that Brown isn't perceived as a lousy teammate, but a responsible one for trying to produce the mindset that would lead to his best performance at the most important point in the season. What a moment for mental health.

Athletes in our society are metaphors for strength and success. They touch fans who relate to these athletes, in all sports, as a better version of themselves. In a 2015 TED Talk, performance coach Reed Maltbie made distinctions between developing warriors, not winners. The winners were focused on accomplishments and external goals. They wanted trophies for winning, and at worst trophies for participation. Warriors, on the other hand, are learning how to compete. They are driven by inner purpose and commit to values and not just success. Warriors have a process-oriented growth mindset, compared to winners, who have a fixed mindset. This difference is key in maturation and learning for all athletes or individuals in any field. The development of warriors and not winners was on stark display at the 2023 Ryder Cup in Rome.

During that Ryder Cup, I had clients on both the American and European teams, which means I had access to both team rooms. The differences were stark. The European room was dimly lit. Spa music wafted through the air. They had comfy beanbags to sit on, and Bose headsets to play a meditation or an inspiring podcast. They had acupuncture and leg compression devices. They had inspiring speakers. They gave their players $10,000 credits at one of the most beautiful stores in Rome, where they could take their significant others. The European team rode in buses and sang songs. The American team rode in private cars or buses and checked their individual phones. The Europeans displayed a growth mindset that was process oriented. They had four first-time players and used that to develop both the growth mindset for the team as well as for future teams.

Did Europe win the Ryder Cup because it had all those perks? Who knows? What we can say with confidence is that this was an acknowledgment by the Europeans that mindset and mindfulness could lead to good golf. They didn't put a stigma on taking care of their minds. They didn't shy away from it. They leaned into it. We could all learn from that approach.

Over the past twenty-five years, there have been so many baby steps that have helped taking care of our mental health become more accepted. The PGA Tour now recognizes and supports May as Mental Health Awareness Month. In addition to making public service announcements with players speaking about the importance of tending to their minds, they promoted the work of the Grayson Murray Foundation. That's huge. The foundation, started by the late Grayson's parents, focuses on addiction. Grayson Murray struggled with alcoholism. But it also acknowledges that Grayson Murray took his own life.

The National Institute of Mental Health reports that the age-adjusted suicide rate rose from 10.4 per 100,000 in 2000 to 14.2 in 2022. Among males, the numbers are higher: an increase from 17.7 to 22.9 per 100,000. The numbers are frightening. What happens with suicide is people always—always—feel like they didn't do enough. They think they could have helped the victim. They think they could have saved him. So talking about suicide after the fact can both help the people who lost a loved one understand it's not their fault and also lead to a greater understanding that any stigma around mental health should have long since been buried.

According to the 2023 United States National Survey on Drug Use and Health (NSDUH), 48.5 million Americans over the age of twelve met the criteria for drug addiction. This is approximately one in every six adults, and it translates into every occupation. It's difficult to say conclusively how common this would be with professional athletes, given their emphasis on fitness, but combined with the stressors on the PGA Tour or in other professional leagues, it wouldn't be surprising to find that the rates are the same.

In 2025, not long after that PGA Tour official wondered aloud to me about whether anyone would use a mental health trailer, the tour hired a therapist to be at tournaments. The mental health program in prior years offered a website from which players could get materials and was also a clearing house for finding practitioners. Placing a mental health professional at some of the tournaments was a logical next step. The idea, as it was explained to me, is that this person— whose credentials are impeccable—would sit in the family dining area that is off-limits to the general public and encourage people to talk to her. The consensus among people I have talked to—players, agents, caddies, you name it—is that if the tour was worried that no one would walk into a mental health trailer, why would they think a player would feel comfortable starting a relationship with a mental coach or therapist in the middle of a room crawling with their competitors and their families? It's so clear to me that that's not the model.

But what is? I started thinking about what a mental health trailer would look like. Of course, it wouldn't be all about golf, but there could be a simulator so players could take some swings and measure everything they want—ball speed, spin, trajectory, etc. There could be brain-wave readers so they could get a read-out of what they're feeling when they hit a shot. There could be headphones loaded with podcasts about mindfulness, books that deal with performance and anxiety. It should be comfortable and quiet, safe and relaxing. And we should work to make sure no one is ashamed to walk in there. It should be a gym for the development of our minds and spirit, as well as a resource for contact info if any sort of crisis is happening to a player, team member, or anyone involved in the golf tournament.

To do this, we have to educate. In professional golf, and in society. We have to get people to assess and admit how they're feeling. We have to provide people with tools to deal with their issues. So many PGA Tour players are millionaires multiple times over. They can pay for help. As we begin to more widely discuss mental health, I think a lot about access. We should make sure people of all socioeconomic levels are aware of what's available online for free. We should inject this discussion into our public education.

Just as we must assess and understand our own situation from all angles, we must assess and understand where we are as a society. We can fill our toolboxes with tools that help us focus and execute on the golf course, and that can lower our handicaps and help win tournaments. But we have to lean into the idea that it isn't just about the golf. It's about our relationships and our habits and our behaviors. It's about our *lives*. There should be no stigma attached to living the best version of our lives, to being our best selves. We shouldn't be embarrassed by that chance. We should embrace it.

Chapter 13

# Grief

*"If we climb high enough, we will reach a height from which tragedy ceases to look tragic."*
—Irvin D. Yalom

*"What we lost outwardly, we often find inwardly—in strength, in wisdom and compassion."*
—Thich Nhat Hanh

We should all be lucky enough to have friends like my husband and I have friends. If you're married and have children, you probably know exactly the sort: The people whose kids are roughly the same age as yours, with whom you split school car-pool duties and then report back on the intimate details the kids share with each other in the back seat, stuff about their lives you wouldn't hear if you weren't quietly sitting in the front pretending to mind your own business. The people with whom you have common values about careers and parenting, work and home, and the balancing act it takes to be successful—or even competent—at it all. The people with whom you travel. The people you bond with—over music, over sports, over family, maybe even over golf.

In 2023, one of our friends who we shared all this with was diagnosed with a rare form of cancer. Twenty months after diagnosis, he died. This was not a "circle of life" passing, a full life lived to a logical conclusion at an appropriate age. Our friend was in his early sixties. Though his three children were grown and out of the house, he continued to live a joyful, active, full life. He ran his own company. He traveled. He worked on his golf game. Death came far too soon. It's hard to think about, much less talk or write about. But the reason I'm telling you about this is because he did death really, really well.

What does that mean? Furthermore, what the heck does it have to do with golf? Those are legitimate questions. Bear with me.

When a friend or relative goes through something like this, we all experience grief. That's obvious. But I realized, as I visited with my friend and watched his condition worsen, that grief has a way of building on itself. It compounds. The grief of one situation makes us think back on grief from the past. An impending loss can encompass all the losses gone by. In spending time with my ailing friend, I realized it conjured up the feelings I had when my mother died, which brought up the grief I experienced when my last dog died, which brought up the trauma in my childhood, which brought up the anguish I felt over losing a friend because we no longer got along. Left unchecked, grief can run amok. It can become overwhelming.

What I realized in watching how our friend dealt with death is that grief can be managed, felt, and contained, but only if it's dealt with honestly and in the moment. We must prepare for it. Like a lot of successful people, our friend was very goal-oriented, the kind of person who would write down plans and actually execute them. He exhibited the kinds of behaviors I have described in previous chapters, the ways I encourage my clients to act in order to maximize their performance. He set goals and then took conscious steps to achieve them. He was an extremely intentional person in his life. It turns out that helped him deal with his death.

Once our friend was diagnosed with cancer and faced death, he didn't waver from how he lived. He brought his three children home to talk to them realistically about what lay ahead. He was direct and honest. The kids all worked with therapists and a separate grief counselor. They didn't run from what was happening. They knew what was happening and took steps to deal with it. The family planned the funeral when their father and husband was still alive, not only acknowledging that a service would happen, but embracing how it should be executed. As their father and husband's condition worsened, they were extremely organized with visitors, setting up thirty-minute windows for friends to stop by, managing what he could withstand physically, mentally, and emotionally.

Not everyone could pull this off. The idea, as we go through all manner of experiences—positive or negative, uplifting or tragic—is to make sure we allow ourselves to *feel* things. That includes grief not just after we experience loss, but as we prepare for it. Denial is dangerous. It can make things worse both in the present, when a family member or friend is struggling physically, as well as afterward, when the person passes on.

Now, to golf. I want to be careful here. My friend's experience with his impending death led me to think about my clients and how they deal with various forms of adversity they face in their careers, in a season, in a tournament, or on a given hole. But at the same time, I'm not linking the death of a family member or close friend with an errant golf shot. They're quite clearly not analogous in import or impact. Suggesting otherwise would be silly.

I do, however, think there's an important way to connect how we handle the two experiences, even though they carry vastly different gravity. We have to acknowledge that in golf, there's often far more failure than there is success. That can be true at the professional level in which a tournament— viewed through a certain lens—has one winner and more than one hundred losers. Scottie Scheffler won six tournaments in 2025, including two majors. It was a historic year. But he played twenty events. That means he "lost" far more than he won.

Pros deal with those potential failures all the time. Did they make the cut? Did they move up in the standings enough to keep their tour cards? Did they slide down the world rankings to the point where they're not qualified for majors? Dealing with failure, and the grief that comes with it, is a major part of the job.

Break that down and apply it to our own games. Each round can feature more shots we want back than those we execute properly. We can look at our scorecards after playing and rue the sloppy double bogeys that should have been avoided. String a few bad rounds together, and we start to bemoan the state of our games, wondering if we'll ever play our best again. We've all been there. It feels like failure, and we grieve in ways both tiny and enormous. Or worse, we don't grieve at all.

This is another set of circumstances that needs reframing. If we have ways to identify small areas of progress, even in the midst of struggles, we have a better chance of moving through the grief successfully. What does progress look like? In the midst of a poor round, maybe you chipped the ball quite well. Maybe you made a few putts. Maybe you managed your game and your emotions properly. If we can find little victories in our round, in our day, in our month, in our career, those little victories can mark progress. That progress then offsets the struggles, and then the struggles are less likely to build on themselves and overwhelm you. There's always that one crisply struck iron shot that stands out as the one you want to repeat, the one that brings you back. Carry that single moment as a step forward, even if it's a tiny victory. Rewards create persistent messages in the brain that help us to continue and repeat positive behavior.

In my experience, the people who deal with grief and loss in a healthy, intentional way are usually the people who are more successful. Preparing for grief absolutely helps when that grief arrives. This is true in situations both large and small. We have to deal with expectations. We have to manage logistics. We have to be honest and realistic about the situations we'll face so that we can best take them on when they arrive. Think about how we reframe losing a loved one. A funeral can be rebranded as a "Celebration of Life." When we think about the person who's gone, we might concentrate not on our loss but on how lucky we were to know them and share so many experiences with them. The seeming tragedy of the present can be thought of instead as a lifelong gift.

In psychology, there is real work that has been done on the idea of death and grief dating back centuries. Before we get to that, consider a song by the singer-songwriter Jason Isbell that perfectly applies to these situations, to preparing for grief. It's called "If We Were Vampires." It describes a relationship that's to be valued in the present because, eventually, it will end. It beautifully deals with the finite nature of life. Here's part of it:

> *Maybe time running out is a gift*
> *I'll work hard till the end of my shift*
> *And give you every second I can find*
> *And hope it isn't me who's left behind*

"Maybe time running out is a gift." It's such a poignant thought that emphasizes the importance of the present, of holding hands while we can, of putting forth our best effort in every moment because everything we experience is finite. It acknowledges that there will be an end, but not in a morbid way. Rather, it puts us in a frame of mind that allows us to value what we're doing even though we know it will eventually end. It applies to so many situations. I should concentrate on these final holes of my round, this final putt, because I won't have limitless opportunities in my future. I should put everything I have into this project at work because my clients and colleagues deserve my best. I should value this dinner with my spouse and be present for it because we won't live forever.

Now, the academic element. There are psychologists who believe that much of our distress in life originates with the idea that we don't deal with the fact that we're going to die. Irvin D. Yalom, a Stanford professor and prominent psychotherapist whose quote is at the beginning of this chapter, is among the most adamant proponents of this idea. Among his many books is *Staring at the Sun: Overcoming the Terror of Death*. In that work he writes:

> *[T]he more unlived your life, the greater your death anxiety. The more you fail to experience your life fully, the more you will fear death.*

In another book, *When Nietzsche Wept*, Yalom writes:

> *Live when you live! Death loses its terror if one dies when one has consummated one's life! If one does not live in the right time, then one can never die at the right time.*

Those messages are so important. If you live with the knowledge that you're going to die, and you're not scared of that fate, then you can live much freer and more joyfully.

There's a balance here, of course. We don't want to become so obsessed with the inevitability of death that we wallow in our impending doom. We also don't want to be so hyperaware that bad swings, bad shots, bad holes, or bad bounces are going to happen on the golf course that we arrive on the first tee with a defeatist, negative mindset. Awareness doesn't have to be defeating. It should be enlightening, centering, and freeing.

We've established, too, that the concept of grief doesn't have to apply just to our greatest losses. Lamenting something as insignificant as a lousy golf shot can provide a small measure of grief. But there is so much middle ground here, an area that Yalom dealt with a great deal in his writings and teachings: So many of us grieve time that has passed and worry we haven't lived our best life. It's such an easy mindset to slip into. We want to take conscious steps to avoid it.

I knew someone who was about to turn seventy and was really struggling with the momentous birthday to come. This is a familiar concept. Those nice, round numbers tend to carry outsize significance. In the best cases, we can use them to celebrate with friends and family, treasuring a life well lived—with more to come. But it's also common for people to dread those landmarks. They concentrate not on the wonderful times gone by but on the limited time that lies ahead. If you're turning seventy, you know for a fact you have more decades behind you than decades to come. If you haven't lived your life understanding that—even embracing it—those milestones can be difficult.

I was listening to this person lament his aging, so I asked him if he wanted my opinion. (This was kind of a rarity. People usually seek my opinion. I don't normally offer it unsolicited.) He said he did. So I responded, "I think this is about grief." I could hear him grieving. He grieved the years behind him. He grieved the finite time he had ahead. It seemed obvious to me, and it wasn't an indictment. He's neither the first nor last septuagenarian to react that way to his stage in life.

He was, however, offended. He got defensive. "I'm active. I take care of myself physically. I'm not obsessed with death because I have a lot more life to live."

Maybe he was right. Who am I to say? I do know what grief looks like, what it sounds like. Those experiences—whether it's turning fifty or seventy, etc., or watching a friend die—can really bring on existential thoughts. The famous Austrian psychiatrist and philosopher Viktor Frankl wrote extensively on these concepts, including, "Without suffering and death, human life cannot be complete." Also, consider the following from Frankl, from his book *Recollections*:

> *In some respects, it is death itself that makes life meaningful. Most importantly, the transitoriness of life cannot destroy its meaning because nothing from the past is irretrievably lost. Whatever we have done, or created, whatever we have learned and experienced—all of this we have delivered into the past. There is no one and nothing that can undo it.*

There is so much material to explore in this space. The spiritual teacher and psychologist Ram Dass shares particularly helpful views on death. There's a 2017 short documentary available on Netflix called *Ram Dass, Going Home*. It was made toward the end of Ram Dass's life, which lasted eighty-eight years. It shows him in the years after a stroke took away movement on one side of his body. And it drew on some old speeches, including one in which he said the following:

> *A lot of the fear that death generated that led to denial has gone from me. Death does not have to be treated as an enemy for you to delight in life. Keeping death present in your consciousness as one of the greatest mysteries and as the moment of incredible transformation imbues this moment with added richness and energy that otherwise is used up in denial. Death is not an error. It is not failure. It is taking off a tight shoe.*

What wonderful thoughts. We can combine the lessons of Frankl and Ram Dass and apply them to all sorts of circumstances in our own lives. Be aware in the present. Treasure the past. Embrace the future—a future that includes the end. Don't fight that end. Celebrate it.

◆　　◆　　◆

That's all very heavy stuff. Heavy, but important. Let's get back to the golf course for a minute.

There's a drill used by some people in my profession that is designed to help athletes and competitors prepare for the difficult times they will face. These mental coaches take their golfers in a practice round and deliberately place balls in the worst spots. Maybe it's behind a tree. Maybe it's in the thickest rough, with the ball sitting down. Maybe it's at a yardage that is between clubs for a player who has to carry some water to reach the green, forcing him into both a difficult decision and dicey execution.

It could seem to be a negative way to practice. Why not experience the best feelings as we prepare so we carry those into competition? Rather, this is a way of being realistic. It's a way of acknowledging: These tricky situations are going to happen. This is how you're going to feel. This is how you're going to process and prepare to execute that shot in competition. You know your swing isn't always going to be perfect, and you're going to have to play through that struggle. It's a way to plan for some small failures and set expectations for what inevitably will happen. The important lesson here: It's not what happens to us. It's how we deal with it. We mustn't lament our misfortune. We must master our response to it.

Now, some golfers think this idea of purposefully practicing difficult, even absurd situations is ridiculous. It's not for them. But others really take to it and benefit from it. That's important, too: Learning what works for each of us, because there's no cookie-cutter approach. Try different things on for size and find out what works for you.

Let's take that idea a step further, though. The message here is that preparation is so important at all levels of our lives. When we perform—on the golf course, leading a presentation, whatever the task at hand—we can't be afraid of the situations we face. We certainly can't be afraid to fail. Performing with that mindset is inherently limiting. It's defensive. It goes back to that idea of playing for others, of feeling shame for how we execute a task while people are watching. We can only put on our best performance when we're playing with freedom. We're not scared. We're confident that our preparation will allow us to draw out our best self.

That kind of excellence can't come when we're grieving about what's gone wrong. It can't come out if we're allowing that grief to build on itself. I go back to that idea that when we're frazzled, when we have allowed our minds to slip into a defeatist state, we might think we're driving through traffic and hitting every red light. As we've discussed, that idea translates to the golf course: None of the bounces are going my way. My ball clipped that branch instead of clearing the tree. It bounced weirdly into the rough instead of staying straight in the fairway.

The reality is: You're probably not hitting every red light. You're allowing yourself to *think* you are. It's another opportunity to acknowledge your frustration—your grief—and be pissed and disappointed. But it's also a moment that can be reframed—the next shot is another opportunity—so that the grief doesn't overwhelm you. Walk into every circumstance knowing there will be losses and setbacks along the way, and then you won't be scared to fail or lose—or die.

There's a little bit of a contradiction here. It can be tricky. We want to prepare that we could run into every red light, so maybe we leave a little early to protect against that possibility. But you don't want to play like you're going to hit every red light—or get every lousy bounce—because that's negative and inherently limiting. Figure out how to get back to that growth mindset—or at least neutral—so that the next swing or next meeting is executed freely.

Aging can be so hard. There is a physical element, of course. To an extent, that can be managed throughout our life by how we take care of our bodies. What do we eat? How do we exercise? How active are we? What avocations do we engage in? There are no guarantees, and random misfortune can befall any of us. (I know. I had back surgery. What a process. Ouch.)

But the mental toll of aging can be even harder. When we're realizing we're approaching our last few chapters, we can wallow in grief. It's easy to be overwhelmed by the thought of losing the chance to live more life. We know that we are on the back nine of our lives. Will you see your kids get married? Will you experience becoming a grandparent? If you're a grandparent, will you live to see your grandchildren graduate from college? Read those sentences and think of other experiences. It's easy to see how grieving what might be missed in the future can overwhelm and take control of your present. Especially as we get older, it's easy to see the glass as half-empty. I can see how people can easily slide into sadness rather than joy.

This doesn't have to be about old age. It also relates to the changes we see in our twenties through our fifties. Change and transition involves loss. In our thirties, we might miss what we have in our twenties. Apply that to any decade or generational shift. Embracing the change, recognizing not only your loss but what you could gain, is key to addressing the grief that comes with transition.

I believe strongly that you have to deal with these issues head-on. Draw from the teachings of people like Irvin Yalom, Viktor Frankl, and Ram Dass. If you can accept that death will come find you, you should be able to find a way to live freer and truer to your values—true to your soul's message—

without believing that in the time between now and death you're going to hit every red light. Grief can be good if and when we're prepared for it, if we've trained for its arrival and we know how to deal with it in the moment.

I realize it could seem like a stretch to write about our feelings about grief and death in a book that's supposed to help with your golf game. But if you have made it this far, you must believe that digging deep into our own lives and experiences can only help us improve. That's on the course. That's at the office. That's in our lives, which will include all manner of adversity. Let's review a few ways to apply these massive themes about life and death to all sorts of situations as we go through life.

- **Prepare for grief:** Be aware that difficult circumstances will befall us all. Don't dread them. Acknowledge their inevitability so that when the time comes, you're armed with the ability to honestly navigate the situation. It's the best way to prevent grief from building on itself.
- *Feel*: Denial is the enemy here. Dig into the emotions that surround grief. That could be a major life event such as the loss of a friend or family member. That could be something as trivial as hitting a tee shot out of bounds. Letting out the feelings is the only way to return to a productive growth mindset—or even to neutral.
- **Think about aging, changing failures, and the like:** If growing old and experiencing setbacks along the way are inevitable, why treat them like they can be avoided? Acknowledging that we will turn forty, fifty, seventy, and so

on can help us make sure we're centered in the present, that we're living a freer, more joyful life.

One more thought from Ram Dass: "Death does not have to be treated as a memory. Death imbues this moment with added richness."

In life, we must be aware of death. We just can't be held back by its inevitability. In life, we must not only grieve our loss, but use it to live our most enriched life.

Chapter 14

# Teamwork

*"If you want to go fast, go alone.*
*If you want to go far, go together."*
—African proverb

In most of its familiar versions, golf is an individual sport. Each of us is responsible for our own swing, our own shot, our own score. Even in competitive formats, we're often told to play the course, not our playing partners. There's a certain isolation to the game that can be simultaneously comforting and unsettling—depending on our surroundings and our mindset and what we're trying to gain from the game at a particular point in our lives.

I learned early on during my time working around the PGA Tour, however, that *professional* golf is a team sport. That concept has become more important over the years as teams have grown larger. Players have employed swing coaches going back generations. Now they're more regularly employing mental coaches and sports psychologists. Most of the top players have putting coaches. Most have physiotherapists to help with training and recovery. Some have nutritionists. Some have chefs. They all have agents. Increasingly,

213

players are involving analytics experts to break down their games and help them identify areas that need improvement. Add all those up, and almost every established pro has at least half a dozen people working for him—oftentimes more. A PGA/LPGA Tour player's name is alone atop the leaderboard. It represents a team that helped him or her get there.

The team member I left out from the long list above might be the most visible and the most important: the caddie. It didn't take me long on tour to figure out that most caddies—certainly the caddies on the highest professional tours—do more than carry the bag and provide a yardage. They're not mules. Far from it. The best caddies are completely in tune with their players' emotional and psychological needs for a given tournament or in a certain round or over a specific shot. Yes, caddies must identify the wind and know how much the downhill trundling of a hole will affect the flight of a shot. They need to be involved in picking a target. They have to know their players' stock yardage with every club. But much more important: A caddie needs to completely understand his player's inner state. When does adrenaline pump through his veins to the point that he needs a shorter club? When is it appropriate to offer advice about club choice and execution and when does he need me to shut up? What's a good way to spend time on the range or on the putting green? Yes, please show up on time and with all the necessary equipment. That's the baseline. The best caddies offer so much more. They are an essential part—maybe the *most* essential part—of any team.

Over the years, caddies have become central to my work

with players. They are often my entry point. A caddie is more likely to understand and recognize that his player could use some help with his mental game, quite frequently before the player reaches that same realization. I have had far more conversations with caddies on the front end of a relationship with a player than I have with the player himself. Caddies can provide an unbiased, external view of what a player might need. Plus, their world is more comfortable for me. At a tournament, I often eat in caddie dining, which is separate from where the players gather. At a place like Augusta National Golf Club, you're far more likely to find me in the caddie area at the end of the practice range than anywhere else during the Masters. The caddies and I share so much because we're just there to help our players. It makes sense that we compare notes on what the player might need on a given day or for a stretch of competitive tournaments on the horizon.

The caddie is kind of the forward-facing member of a tour player's team. If you really have a team that you trust, then those team members will likely see you at your worst. In golf, the caddie is almost always the first person who gives a congratulatory hug after a victory, there for the galleries and the cameras to see, but they also have a front seat to the low moments. They see the flip-outs and frustration during a practice session. They hear the horrible self-talk a player issues himself in the middle of a round. They know when a player tries to drink a slew of poor results away. You know how a hairdresser has a reputation for getting dumped on with all the ups and downs of a person's life? That's the caddie, the hairdresser of professional golf.

I bring this up not because you're going to have a caddie who works with you every round—or even have a caddie at all. I bring it up because, as we make our way through our lives, we all have teams. We have teams at work—bosses to whom we have to report, employees we have to motivate to bring out their most productive selves, colleagues with whom we collaborate who demand and deserve our attention and respect. We have teams at home, of course—spouses who help us manage our houses and our finances, our time and our children, our social lives and our emotions. Many of us have teams of friends, people with whom we share time, stories, concerns, and experiences. Golf can seem like a singular pursuit, and for many of us, there's something soothing about that. Yet managing our lives requires teamwork on all levels. There's so much support that we draw from the people around us. Our teammates are essential in every setting. The choices we make about our teams have an enormous impact on our lives. And if we have a team we trust, they will see our dark sides. They won't be shielded from our lowest moments.

One thing I like to do with my players is hold team meetings. Now, this can only happen when I sense they're ready. They have to be equipped—mentally and emotionally—to sit around a table or be in a room with the people who know them best and receive honest feedback. These are the people with whom they have entrusted key parts of their development. They need to be ready to hear from them in an unfiltered way. It's not for everybody, and that's fine. The person at the center of the meeting—in this case, the player, but it could be a boss, a coach, or a parent—must be both mature and secure. But if we have created an environment that is built on trust, if we have created a space where everyone can take feedback in a non-defensive way, meetings like this can be unbelievably helpful. This isn't a weekly pursuit, nor does it have to carry come-to-Jesus weight. Used judiciously, team meetings can be incredibly helpful to my players.

How might we take that concept and apply it to our own lives? I'll meet people—and we all probably know folks like this—who wonder what they should do for, say, their fiftieth birthday? Should I take a trip? Throw a party? Go out for an elaborate meal? Sure. Fine. Go for it. Those are all great thoughts, fun ways to celebrate a milestone.

But I think a cooler way to mark the passage of time is to use those moments to take stock in ourselves. If we're committed not just to growing older (which is inevitable) but to getting better (which must be intentional), then those tentpole occasions could be used to really dig into who we are, what we believe, and where we want to go. It's an incredible opportunity to sit around with your team—your family at home, your colleagues at work, your buddies at the golf club—and say, honestly and openly, "Give me some constructive feedback. Tell me things you love about me. Tell me where I need improvement."

This could seem risky. It could make us nervous, even uncomfortable. But sitting for this type of meeting is really an acknowledgment that you couldn't be where you are without the love and support of the people around you. More than that, it's an appreciation of them. You're telling them you trust them. You're telling them you value their opinions. You're telling them that you're willing to consider their assessments because it might make your relationships stronger. It can be incredibly empowering.

This is nuanced. The time and place must be chosen carefully. The subject can't be dragged into it. Rather, she or he needs to be eager, something more than just a willing participant. They have to open themselves up to being vulnerable. Moreover, the teammates who are providing input must prepare themselves for the meeting. This isn't slinging arrows for slinging arrows' sake. It isn't a roast, though a little humor never hurts. It's essentially a group therapy session that might have uncomfortable moments, but from which all team members can emerge stronger and more committed to the group effort going forward.

In professional golf, this practice can be a little dicey. The player is the center of that universe, the CEO of his operation. Those of us providing feedback—being encouraged to be frank in our evaluations—are also on the player's payroll. Caddies make their living off their players. Swing coaches earn more when they're associated with a stable of highly successful players. I earn my keep through my agreements with players to work on their mental approach to golf and life. There is risk for any of us in telling a player what he does well and what he needs to work on. What if the player doesn't agree, and then loses faith in the team member providing the feedback? You can pretty easily apply that dynamic to a workplace, right?

Still, in so many instances, the risk is worth it. Honesty

rules the day. Team leaders should understand that surrounding themselves with yes-men might seem gratifying in the moment but doesn't come close to serving them in the long run. We established very early on in this book: Vulnerability isn't a weakness. It's a strength. Team members should feel trusted and valued enough to deliver tough messages. Buckle up—but be better for it.

Holding a team meeting could also offer us an opportunity to assess who is serving the team and who isn't. You know the old saying: "You can't choose your family, but you can choose your friends." I can see how that applies to professional golfers' teams really easily. I can see how it applies in an office setting. You can't fire your son who won't do the dishes or your husband who leaves the bathroom a mess. But at work or in social settings, you can really evaluate who is bringing the right level of energy and effort and is working toward your collective goals. And you can honestly dig into who, if anybody, is a drag not just on you, but on the entire operation.

I have some players who excel at the team meeting and in creating a tremendous environment for their team. One particular player not only takes input from each team member but offers individual goals for each person he works with before a season even starts. That's pretty good leadership. He is not only open to criticism from the people who he has entrusted with knowing him best, but he is offering his own assessment of what he needs from them. The leader of the team must learn the strengths and weaknesses, the personalities and preferences, of each team member in order to get the most out of them. Being aware of what each team member is offering, and what each team member *can't* bring, is essential in maximizing the performance of the entire operation. Setting clear expectations for every single person eliminates guessing and allows everyone to pull on the same rope in the same direction.

Now, a word about outsourcing and ownership. PGA Tour players have large teams because they have complicated worlds, a specific craft to refine, and taking it all on themselves wouldn't help them maximize their performance. They're smart to off-load some of the responsibilities and lean on their team to help the various parts of their games and their lives. Ultimately, though, they also have to acknowledge their responsibility for their own actions, their own play, their own results. I have seen players lash out at caddies, complain to their agents, vent at their swing coaches, even blame me for a poor finish or a slump. Is that really what's going on? We are here to help. You are responsible for your own self. That's true in golf. But it's true with your teams at work and at home, too.

With my Center for Athletic Performance Enhancement (CAPE), I am the leader. But in most of my work, I'm a team member. That can be tricky, because in any team environment—in sports or in business—there's a strong likelihood that not all team members get along perfectly with each other. Such arrangements can happen, and they should be treasured. We all know examples of our favorite sports teams that seemed to have perfectly gelled together in a particular season, groups who have chemistry that helped them achieve their goals. They are, of course, outliers.

In golf, the relationships within a team can be fragile. A good team member does her job to the best of her ability with no judgment about the other team members, who by definition have different roles. It's up to the team leader to make sure those roles are defined and separate. But it's also up to each team member to stay in his or her lane. The swing coach wouldn't like it if I told one of our players, "You're bending your left elbow too much," or, "You're not rotating your hips enough." Likewise, I can't have the swing coach saying, "Now, before you get over the ball, I want you to envision sheep jumping over a fence," or whatever. The lines on a team can't be blurred, or the team won't be well-served. The team members should be chosen intentionally, and they should have distinct and clear duties.

Now, we all know even the best teams don't stay together forever. You can think of extremely successful player-caddie pairings that eventually went their separate ways. Tiger Woods and Steve Williams. Phil Mickelson and Jim "Bones" Mackay. There are too many examples to count. Players try different swing coaches. They move on from mental coaches. Needs evolve. People mature. Nothing is permanent. That's okay.

What's important for each of us is to be able to recognize when a team member—when a *relationship*—is no longer serving us. This can be hard, especially with people we have worked with over years and years. We know each other personally. We might be involved in each other's families. We have seen each other go through difficult times and come through them on the other side. Breakups of any kind can be difficult, even if they're just professional. But we have all heard golfers address their changes with caddies, swing coaches, or whoever, and they almost always speak emotionally about moving on. When your lives are intertwined, any separation is going to take some untangling. It can be painful.

Worse than breaking up, though, could be staying together. This isn't about to devolve into couples therapy—though you might remember I started my career in golf by helping a touring pro work on his marriage. Professional partnerships must be viewed in the same clear-eyed way as personal relationships. That's why it's helpful to establish goals for team members so they know expectations. That's why it's valuable for team members to be allowed and encouraged to give feedback. If that kind of communication and trust is established, it can be easier to track in real time when, how, and why a team is starting to fail. In turn, that can make the unraveling a little easier. People aren't blindsided. Indeed, in some ways they might expect it, and the parting could feel more mutual.

I have been part of so many successful teams on the PGA Tour, and I have been let go both when players were performing well and when their performances were unraveling. Sometimes, our relationships simply run their course. I've given all I have to offer. The player has grown and improved—though, of course, not in a linear way. Yet I'll admit: Parting can be hard. I care very deeply about my clients' careers. More than that, I care about them as people. I care about their mental well-being. I care about their families. In so many cases, I know their partners, parents, and children intimately. I have worked with their spouses. I have helped their caddies. I'm extremely plugged in. It's nearly impossible to remain emotionally detached. I can't encourage people to feel what they're living through and then remain stoic and off to the side myself. It's why, when I'm following a client in a tournament, I might pump my fist for a birdie or sadly let my shoulders slump after a poor mental decision. I'm part of the team, and I'm invested.

But there's also part of my job that is extremely isolating. Over the years, I'll admit to feeling lonely on tour. Players can go to dinner with their wives or their caddies. Caddies can pal around with each other. When I go to dinner with a player, it's almost always an informal session. We're eating and chatting, but we're working. That's fine. It's just not socially relaxing. There's no gang of mental coaches getting together over drinks to discuss our clients. First, so much of our work is confidential, we would be violating a trust if we started swapping stories. That's strictly verboten. Second, we all have different styles and methods. We're all trying to distinguish ourselves from one another and establish a reputation that might lead players to us. If I'm known as "Backhoe" because I want my players to dig deep, so be it. That's what I believe in.

The isolation on tour can be true for almost anyone out there. Planes, rental cars, hotel rooms, clubhouses, golf courses. This isn't a complaint. It's a reality. But I've wondered over the years if some of the lonely existence I've felt from time to time stems from the fact that I'm a woman. Think

about it, golf fans: What women do you know of who are involved in the realm of men's professional golf? A television
announcer or two. (Dottie Pepper and I are pals.) The tour
wives and girlfriends. And . . . who else? The great British
champion Nick Faldo employed Fanny Sunesson as his caddie for years—winning four majors with her on the bag—and
Fanny later went on to caddie for Henrik Stenson. She now
does some work for me as a performance coach with CAPE.

The list of women out there, though, is incredibly short.
There's maybe a whole book to be written about being
a woman in a man's world. There probably has been. The
point here, though, is—as we think about who we want to
surround ourselves with—we have to be awake to our own
needs. If we're feeling isolated and lonely, why is that? Who
might we reach out to in order to feel more complete? Are
there people we can touch base with over the course of a
long road trip who might take our mind off our work and
the travel and the grind of our jobs and just allow us to relax?
Those people are essential. They could be seen as our teammates, too.

Any of us who work for ourselves could experience the
same feelings I have when I've been on the road for a long
stretch of work. As my business has grown, one way I've
found connection is by holding meetings with the coaches
and therapists who work with me—not one-on-one, but as a
group. Confidentiality is important here, but we have found
it to be incredibly helpful to gather as a group and bounce
various issues off of one another. We can't say, "My client
Bob Smith is really having trouble at home, and he's wor-

ried it's seeping into his performance at work." But we can anonymously talk about cases with which we're dealing, new circumstances that arise, and get some outside eyes on cases we know intimately. Yes, I know that work meetings can be tedious. However, I find these exchanges to be fruitful. They give me a sense of being a part of a different kind of team than when I'm working with my clients. There may be ways to build collegial meetings into your professional life that aren't necessarily about doling out assignments or establishing responsibilities. They can be collaborations that help make each member feel as if she's an important teammate to her colleagues.

Which gets us to our social circles. One reason why golf is such a wonderful pursuit is because of the relationships we build and nurture through the game. We all know how a regular golf foursome can feel like a team. Even if we're competing against each other or just playing for fun, the dynamics are well established. We know who can take ribbing and who can't. We know who will melt down after an errant shot and who will laugh it off. We know who's the best player and who's the worst and which shots should be congratulated and which should be ridiculed. There's shared history, maybe even with trips. It's an important bond.

I have a friend who plays a weekly round with the same foursome. This group—from a variety of backgrounds—has played together for several years. What they don't share professionally, they make up for in stories about kids, sports, or their own miserable golf games. They compete for a few bucks each week, swapping teammates every six holes. Just as for so many of us, that tee time is one of the things they most look forward to each week.

Recently, though, one of the members of the foursome was violating the vibe of the group, if there is such a thing. He was constantly running late to the tee box, so much so that the other members started telling him they had booked a time ten minutes earlier. He caught on to that strategy. It was not uncommon for three of the players to be standing on the first tee—already loosened up, peg in the ground—only to watch the fourth stumbling in from the parking lot, last to hit because that was the only way the group wouldn't hold up the rest of the day. This player also regularly had a business call during the round. He played with his earbuds in, was silent for long stretches, but then might fall behind the rest of the group when it was his turn to take part in his virtual meeting.

For a while, the rest of the group laughed it off. They gave the fourth player grief when he dropped the call. Over time, though, his chronic tardiness and lack of presence wore on them. Eventually, the three of them wondered aloud: "Do we have to play with this guy?"

Our free time is our free time. It can be scarce, so it must be valued. Our relationships with friends or golf partners might not seem as important as those with our family or at work. Still, they're real, meaningful, and impact how we feel about our day or our week.

Breaking up with a golf partner might not seem as hard as getting out of a business relationship or an unhealthy marriage. In each, though, the same rules apply. If we're frank

226

with the people in our friendship circle or our foursome while we're growing annoyed by their behavior—indeed, before we snap—we have a better chance of salvaging the relationship and remaining teammates who enjoy one another's company. My friend and his group could have been more intentional in addressing their partner's tendency to be late. "Hey, man, that's three weeks in a row, and you're putting us in the spot of holding up the rest of the groups behind us. Could you leave a little extra time?" They could have addressed his business calls and the impact on their round. "Jim, we know you want to do both, but if you have an hour-long call, couldn't you be honest about it and play on a different day?" Failing to talk to our teammates in real time can make expectations fuzzy. By the time my friend and his group confronted their fourth, his behaviors were so ingrained that he thought they were accepted. He was surprised to find there had been anger bubbling beneath the surface. No one was happy.

Who we surround ourselves with matters. If we're a leader at work, we make choices about who's on our team. Let's review some steps that can make us function better within our teams:

- **Communicate:** Whether you're a team leader or a member, it's important that expectations are established in the present so that there's less risk of disappointment or failure at the end of a project. Team leaders should provide clear responsibilities to their underlings. Employees should articulate what they need to best perform their jobs.

- **Be vulnerable:** This is one of our most important strengths. Allow your team to assess your performance. Listen, don't judge. Be open, not defensive. Hear where you could improve. Trust that the feedback is honest— and that if you take criticism in a constructive way, your team members are more likely to do the same.
- **Be choosy:** Understand who is stealing energy and light from your life. Be honest about what each person around you offers. Give feedback to those who are sapping you of what you need so that they're not caught off-guard, and so that you don't confront them with anger.

What we're really talking about with teamwork is relationships. All of our relationships—familial, professional, social—affect us. They should be treated as important. But they also should be acknowledged as living, breathing organisms that evolve.

I have often said to players that I want to help them. But even as I have them set goals for themselves, I tell them I have a goal for the entire process: My goal is that you get to a point where you don't need me anymore. The goal for a team isn't to stay together and stay the same in perpetuity. The goal for a team should be that all the members grow and become the best version of themselves.

# Chapter 15

# The Gift of Golf

*"Golf is like life. You get bad breaks from good shots,*
*you get good breaks from bad shots, but you have to*
*play the ball where it lies."*

—Bobby Jones

A few years ago, I was invited to serve on a panel that spoke before members of Congress as part of the celebration of National Golf Day. The occasion is typically a lobbying effort by the golf industry to help promote the game and its benefits to the entire country by taking advantage of a forum on Capitol Hill. This "lunch and learn" session, as it was billed, had an interesting title: "Championing Golf. Championing Minds. Championing Communities."

I was joined by Len Mattiace, a two-time winner on the PGA Tour, and Dr. Jessica Gomez, the executive director of the Momentous Institute, a nonprofit organization that focuses on the mental health of children. Alex Baldwin, president of the Korn Ferry Tour, served as the moderator.

This session was not what might be typically highlighted on National Golf Day—the economic impact of the game or the increasing number of participants, statistics that show

how important golf is to our society. It was not a congressional golf clinic. This session fell in May, which has been designated as National Mental Health Month. The opening remarks came from a member of the Congressional Mental Health Caucus. Participants watched a screening of the Netflix documentary series *Full Swing*. The episode was entitled "Mind Game," and it featured Wyndham Clark's march to the 2023 U.S. Open title and the work Wyndham and I did behind the scenes to prepare him for that moment. Wyndham's success with mental coaching was contrasted with the failures of Joel Dahmen, who was reluctant to seek help. I was asked to come prepared to talk about the reasons golf was *good* for mental health.

Think about that. It's important for all of us to remember. Golf can be maddening. It can be frustrating. It's impossible to perfect. It can drive you to seek help to deal with all the gremlins it releases in your head. It can lead you to pick up a book to get tips on how to overcome the mental obstacles that the game produces for anyone who plays it!

This hearing was an opportunity to acknowledge all the good the game of golf does for us. I made a list of all the benefits. Golf can provide exercise and afford us time outside in nature. That seems obvious. (Leave the cart at the clubhouse.) It teaches the adherence to and the importance of rules. It can help kids—and adults, come to think of it—learn accountability. If we approach it the right way, it can serve as a stress relief from the rigors and pulls of day-to-day life. It can help us learn the importance of setting goals and intentionally working toward improvement, which can in turn be applied to other areas of our lives. For those of us who are disciplined about it, golf can provide a four-hour chunk of our day in which we put away our phones and actually become present in our surroundings and with our playing partners. It can help us learn to be present in other areas of our lives as well.

The more you think about it, golf isn't a burden. Golf is a gift.

That should be the lesson here. Through all the digging into our pasts and examining our lives, through learning how to avoid judging ourselves and instead to arm ourselves with tools to deal with our shame and our anger, through managing pressure and confidence and anxiety and learning how to return ourselves to our best competitive mindset—*to be the best version of ourselves*—golf can and should be an ally, not an adversary.

There's a popular idea that our relationships hold up a mirror for us to learn about ourselves. I say versions of that to clients all the time. Think about how you relate to your family and your friends and your colleagues. What does the way you treat them and the way you react to them say about how you feel about yourself and how you live your life? It's an important area to explore.

We also have a relationship with golf. There's a reason why so many people look forward to the round they get to play weekly (or, if you're fortunate, more often than that). It's not just anticipating hitting a driver off the first tee or playing your favorite par-3 or getting a hot dog at the turn. Golf can be a sanctuary and a respite. It can be a distraction and a diversion. It can challenge our bodies and our minds. It tests us in different ways every round, every hole, and every shot. Those are great qualities, reasons that golf is a gift.

But if we have a relationship with golf, then that relationship holds up a mirror for us to learn about ourselves, too. Just as with our relationships with people, we must tend to and work on our relationship with golf so we can learn as much as we can about so many aspects of our personalities and our lives. How we react to adversity. How we handle success. How we deal with our anger. How we respond to bad luck. We often say that a certain golf course tests our game in a specific way. We might generalize from there and say that the game of golf tests us in ways that are almost limitless.

At a time when it's fair to worry about how we relate to one another in our country and across our planet, golf can provide a venue to do just that. Golf can provide a common language for people of all belief systems and backgrounds. It's such a great starting point for building what we lack right now: relationships with people we don't know.

I was on a flight recently, and I noticed something that we have all probably experienced. From the time I gathered at the gate with the other anonymous passengers, then boarded the plane, then found our seats, then took off and traveled to our destination, then landed and got off the plane, no one talked. Not a single peep. Everyone at the gate stared into their phones. When we were on the plane, people watched movies or shows they had downloaded or bought the Wi-Fi package so they could keep in touch with their friends on the ground. There was no, "So, where are you from?" Or, "Oh, you're an Eagles fan? So sorry about that." Or, "What do you do for work? What brings you to Memphis (or wherever)? Have you tried such-and-such restaurant?" The flight was completely silent from start to finish.

This is an old person's gripe, of course, and it seems like I'm longing for a simpler time. Maybe I am. But I also think our decreasing communication is real, and I worry about it. What's going to happen to our relationships with other human beings as technology continues to creep further and further into our lives? We spent some time earlier in this book talking about the stigma of dealing with mental health and how that is slowly eroding. Even if we have a long way to go, we have come such a long way. Thank goodness. The congressional event is an example of that.

Yet as tending to our mental health has become more widely accepted, and as professional golfers have routinely made mental coaches members of their ever-expanding teams, there is a risk that we are watering down the work that we really need to be doing. That work can't be cursory or done in half-measures. We can't pay lip service to it. It must be consistent. It must be serious. And it must be based in the relationships we have established—perhaps with a therapist or mental coach, but certainly with our close friends, family, and, of course, ourselves.

Over the course of the 2024–25 PGA Tour season, I must have heard of a dozen plans from people in the golf world— current players, former players, people on the fringes, agents, and everyone in between—who were hoping to develop apps for our phones that would help us with our mental health and then apply that to our golf games. At some level, it makes sense: We get news, entertainment, recipes, and correspondence through our phones. Why not treatment for mental health? My guess would be that within a couple of years there will be a rash of apps trying to provide these services. Famous golfers will endorse them. Some will use them. Some might even develop them.

In the course of exploring these possibilities, I have talked to investors and developers from Silicon Valley who think this is a great idea and would like people in my profession to buy in. It makes sense: Get a well-known golfer and his less-well-known mental coach to promote an app we can download to our phones that will provide all the services the golfer pays thousands of dollars for? I can see people saying, "Sign me up!"

Yet I keep thinking about the virtual assistant that helps book Amtrak reservations. Her name is Julie. (The irony is hardly lost on me.) She's not real. She's generated by artificial intelligence. She performs simple tasks: Can I book you a new reservation? Do you have to change an existing reservation? It's an efficient process. As it pertains to train reservations, she does her job.

That's what these developers keep telling me about their plans for mental health apps. These aren't simple guided meditations, the kinds of devices I encourage my clients to use as they start exploring various ways of improving their mental health. The developers want a virtual Julie to help with anxiety, anger, performance, pressure, confidence, all of it. They have said to me over and over: "Julie, AI is going to learn to do what you do."

Now, I'm torn here, because as we've discussed, access to mental health services is a huge issue. If apps are a more affordable and available way to get tools into the hands of more people from all socioeconomic backgrounds, then there's a positive side to their development. I don't want to be dismissive.

But I have reservations. Deep reservations. I think about the psychologist Carl Rogers, who extolled the virtues of something he called "active listening." Here he is writing in a paper by that name—"Active Listening"—with a colleague, Richard Farson, in the late 1980s:

> Listening brings about changes in people's attitudes toward themselves and others; it also brings about changes in their basic values and personal philosophy. People who have been listened to in this new and special way become more emotionally mature, more open to their experiences, less defensive, more democratic, and less authoritarian.

That resonates. It's potentially transformative. It's based in interaction between humans. Apply it to whatever portion of modern society you see fit. But I ask: Is an app going to replace the benefits—for both speaker and listener—of that kind of conversation? I just don't think so. Our relationship with an app just wouldn't hold up a mirror that helps us learn about ourselves in the way our relationship with actual people can. Artificial intelligence may learn tendencies and personalities and be able to respond with what seems like sage advice. I'll never believe it can replace the real relationships we establish when we truly listen to each other. That's between a client and a mental coach or therapist, because I certainly have to be an active listener with every one of my players. But it's also between regular people with whom we're close.

Which gets us back to the golf course and the gifts we find there. Why do we feel like we get to know someone better when we play a round of golf with them rather than when we, say, share a meal? It's not just that golf takes longer. Golf reveals us in ways conversation can't. Yes, at a dinner with two couples, maybe the back-and-forth over a five-course meal might allow us to delve into subjects a little deeper—current events, families, shared experiences, what have you. We certainly can get to know each other—we certainly can listen to each other—just by spending quality time and sharing quality conversation. That's important.

But when you play a round of golf with someone, there's an honesty baked in that is unshakable. There's no hiding. You're naked. At dinner, a participant might be able to overstate their professional accomplishments. On the golf course, overstated ability is immediately revealed. Whether they know you or not, your playing partners are exposed to so many characteristics we have discussed in this book and this chapter—how you handle adversity or success, how you deal with anger or elation, whether you can perform under pressure and stay focused on what's ahead of you. There is a human connection in a round of golf that is becoming rarer in the 2020s. That connection is built on the shared experience, sure. When we step to a tee box, each of us faces the same challenge, and we all must tackle it in the way that suits us best. But the connection is also built on the idea that after we hit that tee shot, we just might walk up the fairway and say to one of our playing partners, "How are the kids? What's up with the new job? How are your vacation plans coming?"

That all seems trivial. Maybe it presents as small talk. But if we're actively listening, there's nothing small about that kind of chitchat. Golf gets us engaged with the next hole and the next shot. It can also get us engaged with each other. What a gift that is.

The decorum and etiquette involved in golf can also be instructive, a gift in turbulent times. We don't hit into the group in front of us. We don't talk during each other's back-swings. We don't step in the line of a playing partner's putt. We play in order of who's away. When we're done with a round, we take off our caps and shake the hands of everyone who's in the group. Maybe that's all trite. To me, it seems civil.

I was thinking about this as it relates to the 2025 Ryder Cup at Bethpage Black outside New York City, on Long Is-land. The competition between the European and American teams was intense, as it is every two years. Europe built an enormous lead over the first two days before the Americans stormed back in Sunday's singles matches.

Ultimately, Europe won. The tournament was riveting. Golf's civil norms, though, broke down. We had been granted the gift of an anticipated competition between two talented, committed, and worthy teams playing for something greater than themselves. What we were left with was boorish behavior from the crowds, who lobbed personal and crass insults at the European players. The public address announcer on the first tee exhorted the crowd—already riled up—to chant vulgarities at European star Rory McIlroy. That's not listening to each other. That's shouting at each other. We should use golf to rise above that kind of behavior, to highlight our similarities rather than emphasize our differences.

Golf should provide a community. We're all trying to improve. We're all dealing with versions of the same issues. We all understand that the mental aspect of the game can be more important than the technical parts of our swings. We should share in those commonalities.

Which is really part of the message I wanted to deliver at that National Golf Day congressional event. It's great that members of Congress thought it was appropriate to highlight the importance of mental health for all of us, whether we have ever picked up a golf club or not. That's a forum that would not have been provided in recent years.

What's most interesting, though, is what happened after our panel spoke to the crowd. There were all these members of Congress and their staffs milling around. They got to talking—people from both sides of the aisle—not about their differences or the issues they were dealing with in government. They spoke about golf.

These Democrats and Republicans realized why they were there and what they shared, which was a love of the game. And literally, right in front of us, a dozen of them who had never played with each other and didn't even know that their counterparts played the game made tee times with each other for that Sunday. I don't know the outcome. I don't know how they fit together. I can say without question—without knowing anything about their games or their personalities— that they learned about each other that weekend. They probably learned about themselves, too. What a gift.

Winning your mental game doesn't involve deploying a bunch of easy tricks that help lower your scores instantly. If you're looking for something like that, you have come to the wrong place. If you have made it this far, you know that by now. Truly improving—as a golfer and a person—involves holding up that mirror and learning about our relationships with other people, with ourselves, and with the game of golf. The journey can be hard. It can also be fun. We must be aware of the value of digging deep into our pasts and understanding how they inform our present. We must be aware of our behaviors, what they're rooted in, and how they affect both ourselves and those around us. We must understand how circumstances impact us, and how we can best be equipped to deal with them in the short- and long-term.

All of that is important, both in golf and in life. If you picked up this book, though, it's almost certainly because you are a golfer. What a club to be in. We speak the same language. We know the same challenges. We battle the same demons. Talk about them. Share them. Revel in them. Get better because of them. We are a community just seeking to get better, bit by bit.

If you take anything from all the words that preceded

these, I hope it's that you have a better understanding of how to enjoy yourself, enjoy your playing partners, enjoy the weather, the nature, and the holes before you. I hope you have a better understanding of not just how to fill up your toolbox with the tools you need to improve your game on the course but also for your life and relationships off of it. I hope you have a better understanding of how you, as an individual, can come to enjoy the game of golf itself, and how you can use it to propel yourself forward at work and at home. The challenges of golf will never go away. The frustrations will surface in almost every round. We might pull our hair or slam our club (infrequently, I hope). It might bring us to our knees. But we have to know that if we dig deep and work, we can improve to the point where we win our mental game more often than we lose it. If we do that, we'll always come back to a centering, calming place. That applies to the middle of a round on the course. It applies to the middle of a project at work. It applies to the middle of our lives, as we press onward, trying to get better, trying to *be* better.

Golf is a lifelong gift to those who play it. Its lessons are legion. Aren't we lucky to take it on? The gifts it shares with us and the gifts it brings out of us can be a vehicle of personal transformation if we have the courage to listen.

# Acknowledgments

I want to start with the most important contributor to this project, Barry Svrluga. His intellect, kindness, humor, patience, and perseverance have been catalysts for this project from its inception. Our long talks began on some fairway around twenty years ago. I want to thank the team at Simon & Schuster and Avid Reader Press, headed by my editor and publisher, Jofie Ferrari-Adler, and my attentive agent, Farley Chase, for their ferocity and encouragement to write the best book I could.

I want to thank my two amazing children, Hana and Noah, as well as my loving and supportive husband, Rick. Thank you three for your unconditional love and inspiration. I want to thank my entire extended family, including my brother Bob, and my sister-in-law Francyn Sacks. I want to thank my girlfriends (you know who you are) and my guy friends (I hope you know who you are), colleagues, players, caddies on the professional golf tours, and the sportswriters who have helped to bring the story of athletes and mental health to the forefront of public awareness. I want to thank my team at Center for Athletic Performance and Enhancement (CAPE) for their forward-thinking and clinical support. It is rewarding to have you surrounding me as we spread the importance of mental coaching with athletes and businesspeople around the world. I want to thank my clients over this twenty-five-year journey who continually teach me how to be a better coach. There is nothing more satisfying than seeing you achieve your dreams.

I want to thank my spiritual guides, professors, therapists, evolutionary astrologers, and researchers for keeping track of me, encouraging me to continually have self-compassion and the courage to keep working on myself. All of you have helped me to look in the mirror and choose to dig deep and then to dig deeper.

I would like to throw a bone to all the dogs that I have loved: Mitzi, Tosh, Bones, Buddy, Daisy, the fiercely irascible Charlie, and Hana's newest pup, Latte.

The book is dedicated to Tim Rosaforte. He was an award-winning journalist for Golf Channel and a senior writer at *Golf Digest* who died of Alzheimer's at age sixty-six. Tim was the first journalist to give my work a voice with loving kindness and his own keen observations. He endlessly showed a willingness to break through the stigma of mental health in athletics. Tim would do meticulous research and ask me detailed questions, and he'd always check on the wording of the insights from our talks before publishing. He dug deep and provided me a path both in golf and through print and television to share my perspectives. He created a public forum in the early days when women were not equally represented in sports. I will always treasure his honesty, professionalism, and kindness. Thank you, Tim.

# About the Author

Julie Elion is the founder of the Center for Athletic Performance Enhancement and has developed one of the premier practices for performance enhancements in golf, sports, and life. She has worked with half of the top ten earners of all time, representing more than $500 million in career earnings, 150 PGA Tour wins, and twenty-five major championship wins over the course of her career. As well as working extensively with golfers, Julie provides mental coaching for business executives, athletes, and teams on both the professional and collegiate level, including in the NBA, NFL, MLB, WNBA, and LPGA.

If you or a loved one are struggling with mental health, please consider reaching out to a licensed therapist, counselor, or medical professional. You are not alone, and support is available.

If you are experiencing thoughts of self-harm or suicide, help is available 24/7 through the Suicide & Crisis Lifeline. In the United States, you can call or text 988, or chat via 988lifeline.org. Trained counselors are there to listen and support you in moments of crisis.

If you are outside the U.S., please contact your local emergency number or a trusted crisis hotline in your country.

Reaching out can be difficult, but it is a powerful first step toward care, connection, and healing.